Simply Dreaming

A COMPILATION OF MY DREAMS

Simply Dreaming

A COMPILATION OF MY DREAMS

Dana Coverstone

Simply Dreaming

A COMPILATION OF MY DREAMS

Copyright © 2023 by Dana Coverstone

All rights reserved. No portion of this book may be reproduced, stored in a retrieval system, or transmitted in any form or by any means, electronic or mechanical, including photocopying, recording, or by an information storage and retrieval system—except by a reviewer who may quote brief passages in a review to be printed in a magazine or newspaper—without permission in writing from the author.

Edited by Keilah Villa
Cover Concept by Keilah Villa

Interior layout and cover design by Uberwriters, LLC.
www.uberwriters.com

Printed in the United States of America.

Scripture quotations taken from the (NASB1995®) New American Standard Bible®, Copyright © 1960, 1971, 1977, 1995 by The Lockman Foundation. Used by permission. All rights reserved. www.lockman.org

ISBN: 978-1-7379918-2-3 Paperback
ISBN: 978-1-7379918-3-0 eBook

Lithos Publishing
80 Living Word Drive
Burkesville, KY 42717
www.danacoverstone.org

Dedication

I dedicate this book to my mother, Clara Coverstone, who passed away in March 2022 at the age of 91. She put up with a lot from me as a very active little boy, stood by me as an adult, and strongly supported me throughout life. Sometime between her birthday and her passing, I went to visit her. She shared a note she had made on February 17, 1978. At that time, I had just turned eight and had a dream the night before. I shared it with her because it troubled me. I didn't understand a calendar I had seen in a dream, and I asked her what 2-0-2-0 was. She explained it to me, then said I told her I dreamed people were wearing masks, lined up getting shots in their arms, and dying everywhere while businesses were shut down. She wrote it down because she said something about that dream seemed profound to her. I am thankful she did, and I am grateful for a mother who loved me with unconditional love. Can't wait to see her on the other side.

Editor's Note

The familiar adage "the book is better than the movie" often sparks hearty debate. Although my dad's dreams were never a movie, most readers first heard his dreams told orally through Facebook or YouTube videos. The challenge of editing this book was to find a balance between the original audio transcripts and the formality of print.

There are noticeable differences between the two versions of each dream. These differences are intentional. My primary goal is to portray my dad's dreams akin to their original depictions while appropriately acknowledging the nuances of written language. It's my hope that my dad's longtime followers find comfort in the familiarity of these written dreams and that his new followers take advantage of the details found in the original transcripts.

— Keilah Villa

Contents

Dedication .... *v*
Editor's Note .... *vii*
Foreword: Understanding the Dreams .... *xiii*
Introduction .... *xix*

Part One: Some Keys to the Dreams 1
Just Go to Sleep 3
Why Pentecost Is a Key to Your Dreams 9

Part Two: Dream Directory 19
The Pandemic 21
The November Fist Punch 23
The Coin Shortage 27
The Attack of the Wolves 29
The Sea Battle 33
An Attack on Speaking in Tongues 37
The Solemn September Assembly 41
The Demonic Sleeper Cells 45
October 2020 49
The Three Assassination Attempts 53
The Final Warning 57
The Emergency Shelters 59
The Harsh Winter 63

Lady Liberty	67
The Tree Grove	71
The Ten Riders	75
The Data Lines	79
Hold Your Breath	83
Benjamin Franklin	87
Abraham Lincoln's Assassination	91
The Church and the State	97
The Birds and the Maul	103
The Plumb Line	107
Biden's Inauguration	111
They Don't Hate Me; They Hate You	115
The Bunker	119
The Mud	123
Air Force One	129
The Elder	131
The Sewer Rats	135
The Flaming Spear	139
The Testing Floor	145
The Watchmen and the Fiery Wind	149
Who Are You?	153
Wall Street Bartering	157
Towers, Chains, and Trains	161
Get Out While You Can and Take Who You Can	165
The Specialist	171
The Desert Road	177
The Three Dragons	181
The Eastern Front	187

The Jets	189
The New Cold War	193
The Rockwell Painting	197
Stopping the Machine	201
The Distraction	205
The Millstone	209
Precision	213
"Hail to the Chief"	219
The Canary in the Coal Mine	223
The Headlines, the Sheep, and the Goats	227
About the Author	*231*
Acknowledgments	*233*
Prophetic Words from the Dreams	*235*
Subject Index	*249*

Foreword: Understanding the Dreams

In Acts 2, the apostle Peter quotes the prophet Joel, who declared that in the last days, God would pour out His Spirit on all flesh, both male and female, young and old. These "last days" began when tongues of fire appeared upon the heads of those in Acts 2 as the Holy Spirit took up residence on the Earth for the remainder of this age. Joel's prophecy and the book of Acts agree that as a result of the baptism of the Holy Spirit and by His inspiration, people would prophesy, see visions, and have dreams in the last days. Time has not gone backward; since then, we are still in the last days, and these same gifts continue. While we remain on this Earth, there will be a need for the gifts of the Holy Spirit to catch glimpses of God's plans. How loving and gracious of God to say that He would not do anything of significance on the Earth without first showing it to His prophets (Amos 3:7). He loves us enough to warn and prepare us for difficult seasons.

Dana Coverstone has repeatedly stated that he is not a prophet, so why is he having dreams to prepare us for this season? I believe this is because he is a faithful, bold, and humble man whom God prepared for this time. And because God chooses whom He will.

There were many dreamers in the Bible who were not prophets: Nebuchadnezzar, whom Daniel interpreted for (Daniel 2); Abimelech, who understood his dream and returned Sarah to Abram (Genesis 20); Mary's husband, Joseph (Matthew 2); and Pharaoh, whom Joseph interpreted for (Genesis 41). Some

Simply Dreaming

dreams, like Abimelech's and Joseph's, are clear and don't need interpreting, while others do.

Where dreams are not clear, it is helpful to have a prophet who can interpret and bring wisdom from God, as Daniel and Joseph did. Many of Pastor Dana's dream videos have interpretations that follow his telling of the dreams. Those interpretations are not comprehensive but give a general overview of the dreams. Since this book contains dreams with little to no interpretation, I felt it would be good to preface it with some basic interpretive principles to help the readers.

1. Dreams are usually symbolic or literal, but usually not both. For example, Mary's husband, Joseph, had a literal dream: the angel told him to flee to Egypt to protect Jesus and gave him another dream to tell him when to return (Matthew 2:13 & 2:19). On the other hand, Joseph in the Old Testament had symbolic dreams of stars and sheaves bowing to him (Genesis 37:6-9).

2. God speaks to everyone differently according to their understanding or calling. Dana's dreams with the calendars were highlighting specific times for prayer initiatives. Dana is a man of prayer, so God highlighted seasons of importance regarding prayer. In his first dream from December 19, 2019, the finger underlined March and tapped the calendar three times. This was when the COVID-19 shutdowns began in the U.S. Then, the finger underlined and tapped June when the riots began and when the next dream would come. The dream on June 22, 2020, had the finger highlighting September, where, in a later dream, Dana was instructed to start a prayer initiative.

3. The vultures in the first dream turn into gargoyles in the next dream to indicate the desire or plans of the enemy. The good news is that when God reveals the enemy's plans, His people can intercede to see the outcome changed. Elisha did this in 2 Kings 6. When an army kept coming against

Israel, God showed him their plans in advance. Elisha would then tell the king when and how they were coming to attack. It did not prevent the attack, but the enemy did not gain victory over God's people.

4. Dreams mature with the dreamer's ability to understand them.
   a. Dana's early dreams told of events, some of which would happen quickly. These were God's way of sending a wake-up call (sickness, hospital overcrowding, riots, coin shortage, etc.). He saw a finger, but not the Man.
   b. Then, his dreams moved from the people to the political. Some of the political dreams appeared to have information for those "in the know" in government. One dream was confirmed by the detailed description of a room not open to the public, which Dana had never seen (The Bunker Dream). The political dreams were also for prayer, as we are instructed to pray for those who have authority over us. These dreams gave us glimpses of issues going on behind the scenes so we would know what to pray about.
   c. Later, the appearance of the Man in the dreams brings focus and instructions to understand the dreams. The Man would say things like, "I told them to pray, but they did not. They need to take it seriously now" (The Distraction Dream). Whatever instructions come from the Man at the end of the dreams should be the focus of the interpretation. In the Distraction Dream, it would be easy to focus on the events in the nations and the plane going down, but in contrast to the terrified people, the Man in the plane was not worried. Therefore, the demeanor of the Man and His words become the focal points of the interpretation. Where there is any question about the dream's purpose and focus, the Man answers with a clear message. Why does the Man appear and

give us clear focus? Because the point of life is to focus on the Lord, to hear and obey Him. Whatever we go through in this life, we should always keep our eyes on the Lord and obey His words.

5. Just because a dream is symbolic and the interpretation calms fears for believers, and just because it's a prayer initiative does not mean we will avoid everything depicted in the dreams. Israel didn't completely avoid conflict because of Elisha's warnings. In Jeremiah's time, everything the nation dreaded happened because they did not repent.

6. I have never said that the dreams would or would not come to pass. Why? Because prayer can change things.

7. God told Moses He was going to kill all the people for worshiping the golden calf they made, but Moses interceded, and many lives were spared—though not all (Exodus 32). Abraham interceded for Lot, and God spared him but still destroyed Sodom and Gomorrah. The fact that God told Abraham His plan in advance demonstrates God's love and mercy and the power of intercession.

8. The reason God uses a prophet to interpret dreams is that, by virtue of their calling, God shows them things to come. The reason I have helped Dana Coverstone is because his June 2020 dream depicted things I had already seen.

Here Are Some of Those Things I Had Seen:

1. In 2012, God showed me that difficult times were coming to the nation. When the birds fell out of the sky in Beebe, Arkansas, I asked the Lord why the schools of fish and flocks of birds were dying in groups all over the world. He took me to Genesis 1, where I saw that God pronounced a blessing on the birds, fish, and man saying, "Be fruitful and multiply" (Genesis 1:28). But He did not bless the trees, vegetation, sun, moon, or cattle this way. I knew then that

a blessing was being removed to some degree, which would affect our food source and economy.

2. In 2014, He gave me a time marker to let me know when it would begin. I had a vision of yellow bananas with a price tag of 59 cents. At that time, bananas were 29 cents at my local store. This told me that groceries would more than double and that difficult times would be coming to the U.S. when bananas hit that price in my local store. I told my church that I did not know what would happen but to watch. It happened the week of March 10, 2020, just before the churches were asked to close due to COVID-19 and prior to Dana's dream going viral in June.

3. In 2015, God showed me foreign soldiers in the U.S. In the vision, a troop of soldiers in foreign uniforms was marching up the hill to remove me from my house. I knew they were going through neighborhoods sweeping people out to relocate them. In this vision, I spoke the name of Jesus, and they all fell flat. I thought the vision was symbolic, showing me that I have God's protection, so when I heard Dana's dream with Chinese soldiers on our land, it really got my attention. His dream caused me to wonder if that could actually happen since I had already seen it. It was a scary thought!

Fortunately, God equipped me for this season so that I would not be too fearful and could help others overcome fear. I will, however, confess that in 2010, fear was my first response. The Lord started preparing me by instructing me to learn dream interpretation. As I began learning, I interpreted a few scary dreams for different people. They had dark, foreboding images of terrible times. In one of those fearful dreams, the dreamer was walking through it, telling those following her to step where she was stepping, and they would "make it through." My prayer became: Lord if I have to go through hard times, let me walk like her . . . in the Spirit . . . unafraid . . . with people following me to

Simply Dreaming

safety, rather than like the two other people's dreams who were running in terror with no certain end in sight.

Many have disagreed with my spiritual interpretations, focusing on the events more than the words the Man says in the dreams. I will not say that the events can't or won't happen, but I know the Lord has promised to make a way where there seems to be no way. His children are called to walk in faith rather than fear. The Bible says that though we walk through the valley of the shadow of death, we don't have to fear any evil (Psalm 23). We can take comfort in His Word by His Spirit. He is the Strong Tower that we can run to and find safety. In many of the videos with Pastor Dana, I encouraged people to put on the mind of Christ; ultimately, it is not about how comfortable we can be but about taking up our cross and following our Savior, Jesus, to the other side.

To the believer, I say: keep the faith, take His hand, and trust the Lord to walk through the valley. To the lukewarm, I say: repent and give your all to Him who died to free you of all sin. To those who don't know the Lord, I say: call on Jesus, and He will give you a new heart and life. Heaven will be worth it all!!!

Cherie Goff
www.goffministries.com

Introduction

If, at the beginning of 2020, you had suggested that by July of that year, over a million people would have watched a video I posted on social media, I wouldn't have believed you. If you had further suggested the video would lead to ministry opportunities, meetings with well-known people in the Church world, and church visits from people representing forty-eight states and fourteen countries over the next two years, I still would've had trouble hearing what you were saying. But that is exactly what happened.

This book is simply a compilation of my dreams since December 2019. It is a quick reference to what happened after I posted a fifteen-minute video for 1,100 friends on a well-known social media site. I now thoroughly understand what the term "viral" means and it has not always been enjoyable. It was truly the beginning of God doing some interesting things in my life, and it introduced me to both praise and scrutiny. I want this book to be a resource and an explanation of how I've handled the dreams and the process by which I share them. I also want to recognize a few people who guided me along the way and helped me remain focused on the will of God in all of it.

I have written a chapter on the importance of dreams in the context of Pentecost, and I feel it is vital that you take it to heart. I also want you to pray through the dreams and gain what you can.

There were times when I fully understood the prophet Jeremiah because of the attacks I faced all around me after the

Simply Dreaming

first set of dreams went public. On that note, let me remind you that I am not a prophet. I am a pastor and more comfortable in that skin. I know who I am, so I'm not trying to be anything else. We are all watchmen, though, and have a job to do. I am also a husband and a father, and I walked through the open door keeping that in mind as well. I've also discovered that some doors God opens for you have both a wonderful and a difficult side to them. But discovery is only possible if you step through the door.

On one last note, this book is not about the interpretations of my dreams. This book is simply to remind the Church to stay awake and to work until Jesus comes. I believe Jesus is coming back soon because the signs are getting clearer and clearer that things are afoot. We see world changes that were prophesied in the Word of God. And the Word does say that in the last days, God will pour out His Spirit on all flesh (Joel 2:28, Isaiah 32:15, Ezekiel 39:29, Zechariah 12:10, and John 7:39). Dreams are part of that spiritual reality, so if you are a dreamer, keep dreaming.

Part One:

Some Keys to the Dreams

Just Go to Sleep

As of the writing of this book, I have been in full-time ministry as a pastor for thirty years. I first served for ten years as the youth and children's pastor in my home church in Jasonville, Indiana. After that, I was a senior pastor in Seelyville, Indiana, for nine years. Today, I'm in my twelfth year serving as a senior pastor in Burkesville, Kentucky. I've been involved with ministerial associations, performed weddings and funerals, counseled people in difficult situations, prayed for people needing wisdom, held the hands of dying members in hospitals and nursing homes, and preached or taught almost every Sunday and Wednesday night since 1991.

Over the course of my ministry, God has used me in the spiritual gifts of words of knowledge, words of wisdom, and discernment. Although God has used me in the other spiritual gifts, this triad is where I feel the most comfortable operating. I share this because I believe dreams are an extension of those three spiritual gifts. This is a foundational part of the story because I believe God still speaks through dreams. In Acts 2, the Holy Spirit fell on those in the Upper Room, manifesting Himself in those as they spoke in other tongues. The crowd outside heard them and thought the people speaking in tongues were drunk. When they questioned Peter, he explained it was the fulfillment of an Old Testament prophecy made by the prophet Joel:

> [17] 'And it shall be in the last days,' God says, 'that I will pour forth of My Spirit on all mankind; and your sons and your daughters shall prophesy, and your young men shall see

visions, and your old men shall dream dreams; [18] Even on My bondslaves, both men and women, I will in those days pour forth of My Spirit and they shall prophesy. [19] 'And I will grant wonders in the sky above and signs on the earth below, blood, and fire, and vapor of smoke. [20] 'The sun will be turned into darkness and the moon into blood, before the great and glorious day of the Lord shall come. [21] 'And it shall be that everyone who calls on the name of the Lord will be saved.'
Acts 2:17-21 (NASB1995)

Peter, citing Joel, confirmed the last days had begun and that prophecy, dreams, and visions would be signs of its beginning. These signs implied God's supernatural hand at work in the lives of Christians and made it clear it would not stop for any reason. The newly established Church would see miracles, and alongside those miracles, God would speak to His people through dreams, visions, and prophetic words. It was about to become an extremely exciting time to live, and it would continue through the coming centuries.

This idea has driven me to preach several sermon series on dreams and visions in the churches I've pastored. I am unapologetically Pentecostal, and I unashamedly want those I pastor to experience the fullness of the Spirit-filled life. The Spirit-filled life includes the promise of Acts 2:17 and the spiritual gifts of 1 Corinthians 12:

[4] Now there are varieties of gifts, but the same Spirit. [5] And there are varieties of ministries, and the same Lord. [6] There are varieties of effects, but the same God who works all things in all persons. [7] But to each one is given the manifestation of the Spirit for the common good. [8] For to one is given the word of wisdom through the Spirit, and to another the word of knowledge according to the same Spirit; [9] to another faith by the same Spirit, and to another gifts of healing by the one Spirit, [10] and to another the effecting of miracles, and to another prophecy, and to another the distinguishing of spirits, to another various kinds of tongues, and to another the interpretation of tongues. [11] But one and the same Spirit works all these things, distributing to each one individually just as He wills.
1 Corinthians 12:4-11 (NASB1995)

Because I've experienced vivid dreams most of my life, I first felt led to develop a sermon series about dreams in the mid-1990s. At that point, I was a youth pastor dreaming a lot about people I knew and the situations they were facing. In some of the dreams, I saw the way out of the problems these people faced. At times, God would show me sensitive things about people, such as sin issues with which they struggled or upcoming battles they would face. In response, I would share my dream with them. The recipients always responded with tears and, often, gratitude.

I began researching dreams from a biblical standpoint and making notes. I started discussing the subject with my youth group and Sunday School class. I was surprised that most were very interested. In fact, some were having profound dreams themselves. As they learned that God speaks through dreams and visions, those teenagers began having revelatory dreams and shared them in my discipleship group. It was a really unique moment of understanding for me. Some of these kids even started being used in the gifts of the Spirit and prophesied as members of the early Church did in Acts 2.

I then began to think of adults hearing the same message and responding to it as well. I began speaking to pastors in my fellowship about dreams, visions, and prophesying and found support. I also talked to specific adults in my church as well as certain friends, to determine the consensus for the awareness of and prayer commitment to receiving spiritual dreams. As often happens with life in general, I got busy with other aspects of ministry, however, and the dreams, although still constant, became more general and seemingly less spiritual. I laid my dream burden down for a long time. I focused on other things, like discipleship and helping my youth group experience more in the Pentecostal realm. It would be another five years before my dreams would become a steady occurrence once more, but I kept studying and researching in the meantime.

In September 2019, I traveled to Egypt with some ministry friends from Kentucky. While visiting the pyramids outside of Cairo, I had an excellent opportunity to ponder the life of Joseph, the dreamer from Genesis. Riding a camel named Sahib, I surveyed the surreal and overwhelming scene before me. I was thinking about Moses and Ramses when the Holy Spirit reminded me of Joseph. That inspirational journey motivated me to create a new teaching series regarding dreams. In October 2019, the inclination increased when a woman in my church (from a non-Pentecostal background) began having dreams and seeing visions. I sensed God wanted to use her in the prophetic gifts, so it became an incentive for me to teach the series on Wednesday nights. Around mid-November, I began dreaming again, this time at an accelerated pace, which is what led to this book you're reading today.

The Visual Nature of the Dreams

My dreams are incredibly vivid and detailed, with deep, crisp colors and clear faces. They tend to be highly complicated and symbolic for both Church and government sectors. I see various countries, world leaders, and conflicts. In the dreams, I see geopolitical, military, and government interests as well as the pastoral aspects of it for the culture in which we live. My dreams also come in flashes, like movie trailers with new bits added over time. Some have recurred for a few nights, while others have recurred for weeks.

The "trailers," just like with movies, eventually add more details and information. When I see the Man who represents Jesus and the Holy Spirit, I either know the dream is nearly over or that it's done. I pray about the dreams once I start having them, make notes, and ask God for wisdom. I identify the distinct symbols in the dream and start researching them for their spiritual, historical, and practical meanings.

I send my dreams to Cherie Goff as soon as I realize they are ones God wants me to share. I arrive at that conclusion based on the repetition of certain elements and my general sense when I wake up from the dream. I simply know based on almost forty years of hearing the Spirit's voice and recognizing God's activities in my life. It is a deep sense to listen and observe what I'm being shown. I liken it to hearing God's voice when I'm preparing to preach a message to a congregation, moved to select certain Scriptures, have sudden revelation, or remember stories that apply to the message itself. I believe the dreams are anointed because when God speaks, His credibility is validated so that there is a response. I believe in the anointing of the Holy Spirit on anything God speaks and on those through whom God speaks. I would be wasting my time preaching if I didn't believe in the anointing.

One of the most important aspects of my dreams is the amount of time spent in prayer before they are presented. Once I have a dream, I share the parts with Cherie, who begins to pray and work through them too. I pray over the dream and ask a select group of others to pray through it as well. I personally spend at least twenty-four hours in prayer for each dream that I share with Cherie, and many times, it's a dozen more hours than that. So, with each dream you hear, you have the prayer investment of me, Cherie, and five to six others.

In total, I can accurately say that at least forty-five to fifty hours of prayer go into each dream before I present it publicly.

Once Cherie and I sense a timeline for presenting, we pick a day and do a podcast introducing the dream. Sometimes I feel an urgency to get a particular dream out sooner, but I trust Cherie's judgment if it's to wait. At times, I've felt led to have her help with the interpretation; other times, I've felt led to not ask her to be involved. I don't always have a specific reason for that; I just try to be obedient.

Cherie is an ordained Assemblies of God pastor and a recognized prophet, which is unique in our movement. She has been trained under Billy Wong, a renowned dream interpreter who has written and presented materials on dreams and dream interpretation. I have complete confidence in her as a friend and colleague. Cherie reached out to me shortly after I released the first dream in order to help me understand the deep waters in which I swirled. I greatly appreciate that she did.

I want to honor God in everything I do that is associated with the dreams because they have profoundly impacted many lives. I also have a spiritual responsibility for that reason. I never shared to cause fear, although that happened initially. I shared the dreams because I absolutely knew they were from God—warnings to the Church at large and to the United States of America. I am not a prophet, but I am a watchman, which is what every wide-awake believer should be every day. As a pastor, I want to feed my congregation and the online audience that follows me with solid spiritual food that will edify them and build them up in their most holy faith. It is time for us to get very serious about our spiritual walk and to work while it is still day. Whether or not you take the dreams seriously, I wholeheartedly do. I must because I know that they were delivered to me by the Lord to warn the Church of what is coming. I have done my best to be obedient in all of it.

That said, I've lost ministry friends even within the Assemblies of God and had local church family get upset and leave. I've been slandered, maligned, stalked, threatened, and viciously attacked on social media, all because I shared what I felt God had shown me. I regret none of it, and I will continue to share dreams that I feel are from the Lord. If my dreams suddenly stop tonight, I will continue to serve as a pastor and a watchman for Jesus until He comes. As you read through my dreams, please pray through them for insight and practical strategy as the world unfolds before all of us in these last days.

Why Pentecost Is a Key to Your Dreams

The Bible is filled with stories of dreamers and their dreams. Several of those dreams have become catalysts for discussion of end-time events and are recognized for their historical precedent and accuracy. Both the Old and New Testaments bear witness to dreams recorded in the Bible that God used to speak to His followers and leaders of nations. While fourteen Old Testament books reference dreams and dreamers (Genesis, Numbers, Deuteronomy, Judges, 1 Samuel, 1 Kings, Job, Psalms, Ecclesiastes, Isaiah, Jeremiah, Daniel, Joel, and Zechariah), only three books in the New Testament do (Matthew, Acts, and Jude).

The first dream recorded in the Bible is found in Genesis 20:3. Here, King Abimelech learns about Abraham's wife, Sarah, whom he had taken as a concubine. Although King Abimelech hadn't touched Sarah yet, in the dream, God warned him not to touch her and explained that He had kept anything from happening between them. Abraham should have stood by his wife in the first place, yet, the fact that God spoke to a king who had no faith in Him indicates that God will speak to whomever and whenever He pleases. This precedent leads to Joseph, who interpreted several men's dreams, culminating in Joseph interpreting the Pharaoh's dream (Genesis 41), and Daniel, who even told Nebuchadnezzar what he had dreamed and interpreted the dream for him (Daniel 2).

Throughout history, kings, leaders, pharaohs, governors, politicians, and scientists have received God-given and God-inspired dreams that impacted their times and the generations to follow. The Old Testament has many more dream references than the New Testament. I believe the reason is crucial for us to understand today and that what happened on the Day of Pentecost is the key to all of it.

In the Book of Acts, those in the upper room prayed in obedience to what Jesus had told them to do, which was not to leave Jerusalem but to wait for what the Father had promised. That promise was a new kind of baptism: "'Which,' He said, 'you heard of from Me; for John baptized with water, but you will be baptized with the Holy Spirit not many days from now'" (Acts 1:4-5, NASB1995). In Acts 1:8, Jesus instructed the disciples to wait for the Holy Spirit to empower them to witness and spread the message He had given them to share: "But you will receive power when the Holy Spirit has come upon you; and you shall be My witness both in Jerusalem and in Judea, and Samaria, and as far as the remotest part of the earth" (NASB1995).

The disciples waited for the power component that Jesus had told them would come. And it did, or rather, *He* did. The Spirit of the Living God came as a mighty rushing wind and appeared as tongues of fire during the Feast of Pentecost when there were many foreign visitors in the city. When the Spirit of God fell on the Upper Room that morning, the disciples began to speak with other tongues as the Spirit gave them the ability. They prayed and praised loudly enough to be heard by the crowd outside. Acts 2:6 tells us that "when this sound occurred, the crowd came together, and they were bewildered because each one of them was hearing them speak in his own language" (NASB1995).

I am unashamedly Pentecostal and pray in tongues daily, but what happened on the Day of Pentecost was more than just about speaking in tongues and exhibiting boldness. Later in the text of Acts 2, Peter realizes the confused crowd thinks that some of them might be drunk due to their volume and strange behavior. Inspired by the Holy Spirit, Peter clarifies that this is undoubtedly of God and confirms it by quoting Joel 2:28-32:

[14] But Peter, taking his stand with the other eleven, raised his voice and declared to them: "Men of Judea and all you who live in Jerusalem, know this, and pay attention to my words. [15] For these people are not drunk, as you assume, since it is only the third hour of the day; [16] but this is what has been spoken through the prophet Joel, [17] 'And it shall be in the last days,' God says, 'that I will pour forth of My Spirit on all mankind; and your sons and your daughters shall prophesy, and your young men shall see visions, and your old men shall dream dreams; [18] Even on My bondslaves, both men and women, I will in those days pour forth of My Spirit and they shall prophesy.' Acts 2:14-18 (NASB1995)

Peter explained the unusual activity with a sound basis from the Word of God. Joel wrote those words around 835 B.C., long before Jesus walked the Earth, died, and rose again on the third day. Peter clearly makes the connection that the baptism of the Holy Spirit and speaking in tongues is the outpouring of the Spirit. Joel also describes it as happening in the last days, so Peter declares that the last days are in effect since Jesus is at the right hand of the Father. In other words, Peter did not tie this event to something that would happen in the future; he said this was the beginning of the days in which the Holy Spirit is poured out into the lives of believers.

There was, however, more spoken by the prophet Joel and preached by Peter that day—that God's Spirit would be poured out on all mankind, every tribe, nation, tongue, and cultural background. God invited everyone to take part in this gift to believers and to be used as His mouthpiece. There were three specific areas:

1. "And your sons and your daughters will prophesy." This includes speaking words that God reveals about future events, declaring who God is and what He is doing among the body of Christ. This was and is to warn others of necessary changes in holiness and righteousness and speaking prophetically with the unction of the Holy Spirit.

2. "And your young men will see visions." God would soon reveal things to the younger men in a supernatural way that only a select few had seen before. Namely, visions expressing what He was doing or was going to do that should be shared with the body of Christ.
3. "And your old men will dream dreams." The American Heritage Dictionary defines dreams as "a series of mental images, ideas, and emotions that occur during sleep.[1]" Joel declared that a time was coming when God would give dreams to godly men who would then share those dreams with the world around them. Dreams would become a way God spoke on the Earth.

Pentecost began the day God said, "I am pulling out all the stops and limitations on who I can use for My glory." Pentecost became the catalyst for a move of God that would change the world because, from that point, everybody could prophesy, have visions, and experience dreams through the indwelling presence of the Holy Spirit. Through the prophet Joel, God had promised these manifestations of His Spirit in and through His people. This was the power Jesus had told the disciples to wait for that would launch them into their callings and introduce supernatural connections from Heaven.

Pentecost was the key to the outpouring of His Spirit on all flesh because the nations were present in Jerusalem on that major feast day. The people witnessed the outpouring of the Holy Spirit with their own eyes and ears. The immediate salvation and baptism of three thousand people after Peter's preaching is evidence that God had shown up and changed the disciples in that Upper Room. The power Jesus promised had indeed come to Earth and was here to stay. People were saved, lives were transformed, prophetic words were given, and visions and dreams would start taking place, as had been foretold by the prophet Joel.

---

1 *The American Heritage Dictionary*. (New York: Houghton Mifflin Company, 1989), 215.

Pentecost was just the beginning. The fire of God's Spirit burned brightly in the hearts of those who spilled out of that Upper Room. The Church was birthed, and the power of God would spread like wildfire through believers in supernatural revelation via dreams, visions, and prophetic words.

Therefore, you cannot separate Pentecost from dreams and visions; they depend upon one another. The Father promises they are a part of the outpouring of His Spirit on all flesh in the last days. Dreams and visions connect through the Father's heart to the filling of the Holy Spirit with the same wind that blows and fire that burns today. Because I'm a Spirit-filled believer (one who speaks in tongues), I believe that my sensitivity is deeper, my ability to listen to the Holy Spirit is more focused, my dreams are more vivid and detailed, and my walk with God is enhanced.

According to Ephesians 1:13-14, the Holy Spirit seals us. But there's an experience after salvation that changes one's walk with the Lord in unfathomable ways. Pentecost changes *everything* by intensifying and transforming all you surrender to Jesus. The power of the Holy Spirit, as it fell on the Day of Pentecost, brought the assurance that dreams and visions were part of God's plan for His people. While some say that God has not moved in this way since the apostles, there are literally millions of others in this day alone who have experienced and discovered that the Father, Jesus, and the Holy Spirit are the same yesterday, today, and forever (Hebrews 13:8).

Jesus made an astounding statement to the disciples that still impacts those reading this chapter in today's world: "Truly, truly, I say to you, he who believes in Me, the works that I do, he will do also; and greater works than these he will do; because I go to the Father" (John 14:12, NASB1995). This promise from Jesus declares that miracles would not cease and that the Holy Spirit, working through believers, would move in supernatural ways through them. The Day of Pentecost was a breakthrough moment for the developing body of Christ because the Holy Spirit spoke through and moved through the people. The Holy Spirit used common and ordinary people to speak of the hope Jesus brings to all who saw and heard Him that day.

God has called us to make a difference in the world, to be a witness wherever we go, taking the gospel to every square inch of the planet. Those jobs would be impossible without the help of the Holy Spirit. That is why in John 16:7 Jesus explains to His disciples that His departure is advantageous to them because He will send the Holy Spirit to guide and empower them. Pentecost became that starting point for the power of God that sent people and endowed them with boldness, gifts, and fire in their hearts. There would be a continued refilling and experience with the fire and power of God to keep people determined, focused, and faithful. The Holy Spirit would be poured out upon the Gentiles as well (Acts 10:44-48), and He would continue to guide Christians throughout the centuries ahead.

I believe that dreams and visions are an extension of the spiritual gifts of the word of knowledge and the word of wisdom (1 Corinthians 12:8). Although dreams were present in the Old Testament, those that occur after the Day of Pentecost—especially in those who are Spirit-filled—have a different emphasis. These dreams are given to provide insight to believers, warn the Church, prepare the body of Christ, and become the extension of His hands to the world.

I firmly and emphatically believe several things: that being Spirit-filled changes the believer for the infinitely better and enhances their ability to use the tools that He gifts us; that God still speaks today through dreams and visions, warning the Church and world of what is coming; that God uses dreams and visions today to shake and wake the Church so that we can share the message of hope and power that is available to us; and that members of the Church ignore the power of God and the gifts in a way they will be held accountable for one day. I could not do the work I do without Pentecost. It makes it possible for me to live in the world where I see through a glass darkly yet walk in His power and authority.

Let me ask some questions: Why do so many people in the Church believe that God stopped moving in miracles, gifts, dreams, and visions after the apostles died? Where did Jesus say anything in Scripture about those gifts and miracles ending? Why would Jesus tell the disciples to wait for something that would only help them get the Church started, then take those tools away and trust the Church to do it all in its own strength and programming? Why would Jesus say we would do greater works than He did but take miracles and gifts out of that reality? How could that be possible? Is there anyone who does not need faith like Daniel in the lion's den? What martyrs do not need the supernatural power of the Holy Spirit to be a witness to those who are trying to take their lives?

I want every tool and gift that is available to me so that I can make a difference, and I wholeheartedly believe that God wants us to have them today. God still moves in Christians in the supernatural, just as He has done through the centuries. God still gives old men dreams and young men visions. I believe that the Day of Pentecost started a fire that still burns like a godly inferno in today's world, and those who are willing can walk in the freshness of that fire at this moment.

Many will disagree with anything or everything I say in this book. But I take Jesus's commission to reach the world with the gospel and what happened on the Day of Pentecost as valid today. Acts 2 and the Day of Pentecost collectively were the launching point of a new way of God working among His disciples. In the Old Testament, the Holy Spirit moved upon men and women of God, empowering them to achieve extraordinary feats like multiplying food ingredients, healing the sick, and raising the dead. As promised by Jesus, the Holy Spirit was sent to Earth on the Day of Pentecost to dwell within us (2 Corinthians 4:7). How could it be that we have the very Spirit of God living within us but at some random point in time He was somehow restrained from continuing to provide the same gifts and do the same miracles He did in the early Church? That simply does not make sense. Pentecost is indeed the key that opened the door to God supernaturally using His people until one day He comes again.

Part Two:

Dream Directory

The Pandemic
December 16, 2019

The dream woke me, and I felt greatly alarmed. In my dream, I saw a calendar open to January 2020. I saw a hand flip the pages to February and March. Its index finger underlined the month of March, then tapped the calendar three times. The calendar flipped through April, then May, and landed on June. The index finger appeared again, underlined June, and tapped three times. Suddenly, the calendar disappeared.

What replaced it was an array of images. I saw groups of people wearing masks, coughing, struggling to breathe, and on ventilators. Hospitals were overwhelmed with long lines and exhausted medical officials. Ambulances flew down the road in a frenzy. Headlines everywhere read, "Thousands of People Are Getting Sick."

State capitals and courthouses began to be surrounded by furious protestors. Angry people marched the streets with clenched fists and guns held up in the air. Major cities were on fire and had barriers erected within them. Vultures flew overhead despite the rising smoke. Every scene was pure chaos. Fearful people hid in their homes, peeking out their windows with guns in their hands. In the midst of it all, I heard a white figure say to me, "Brace yourself, brace yourself, brace yourself."

The November Fist Punch
June 22, 2020

A calendar and the same white figure appeared. I now felt that it represented God the Holy Spirit. There was nothing evil or sinister about the white figure; instead, it was pure, righteous, true, and holy. The Holy Spirit (the White Figure) said to me, "Part two, part two."

The calendar began flipping through June, July, and August 2020. When it hit September, the calendar stopped, and an index finger appeared, tapping the month three times. Then the calendar flipped through October and stopped to underline November. Suddenly, the hand balled into a fist, reared back, and punched November. The calendar caved back into the wall, its numbers flying off the pages in 3D as if they were no longer attached. It was a very destructive act, one of the most graphic parts of the dream.

I immediately saw people protesting and fighting in the streets. Businesses were shut down, and classrooms had cobwebs hanging in them and posters falling off the wall like no one had been in them for months. I saw the roofs of banks open, and money was being sucked out as if by a vacuum cleaner. As this happened, I sensed it was a transfer of wealth. I saw politicians in back rooms patting people on the back, laughing, and smirking as they made deals with each other. I saw that Washington, D.C. was on fire outside. Monuments in the city burned and blazed; fires were everywhere.

I saw Chinese and Russian soldiers working alongside blue-helmeted United Nations workers. The Russian soldiers would tell the Chinese soldiers to round up people and secure certain quadrants. Despite all the military activity, I saw no sign of President Trump or leadership in Washington, D.C.

The vultures now appeared to be gargoyle-like, and instead of circling high above the cities, they were circling ten to fifteen feet above the ground and attacking people. Then there were more flashes of explosions all around the nation, larger protests, and more violence. People were hiding in their homes in fear, watching homes and churches being burned.

The White Figure appeared before me and said, "Brace yourself, brace yourself, brace yourself."

At that moment, I woke up. My Fitbit indicated my heart rate was at about 180 beats per minute. It came to me that this was part two of the dream I had in December 2019.

The Coin Shortage
June 23, 2020

As I approached the local bank to get quarters, I saw a sign on the door that said, "We have no change." Even though I took note of the sign, I still walked in anyway. The bank's president was at a teller station. I walked to her station and asked, "Can I have $10 in quarters?"

"I'm sorry," she replied. "The bank no longer has coins because the Federal Reserve is no longer minting any."

"So, how can I charge $1.50 for something?" I asked her.

"Prepare for hyperinflation and just charge $2," she explained. "And by the way, $1 and $5 bills will soon follow."

And again, I heard those words, "Brace yourself, brace yourself, brace yourself."

The next day, June 24, in waking life, signs started going up around the nation concerning the shortage of coins in financial transactions.

The Attack of the Wolves
June 25, 2020

It was night, and I looked down at a field full of dark, sleeping wolves. A figure that was covered entirely in black came rushing in. I couldn't see the figure's face, color, or race. It looked almost like a ringwraith from *The Lord of the Rings*, and it held a large whip with what appeared to be a metal bolt at the end of it. The figure began whipping the sleeping wolves until they were in a frenzy of pain and hostility. The wolves growled at their attacker but did not approach or threaten him. It became clear to me that he was their master. As he hurt them, their eyes began to glow red like LED lights. They all growled and bristled as they gathered around their leader. He turned counterclockwise, pointing in all directions until he came full circle. "Go into the cities," he gruffly instructed. The wolves took off, running as fast as they could in all directions, growling and nipping at each other.

The scene changed to a room where one wall was a giant video screen of smaller screens. On the screens, I saw pastors, missionaries I knew, and others I didn't. I saw men and women of every race, color, and nation preaching a hard, aggressive gospel. The more they preached, the more they became drenched in sweat. Something like smoke or a cloud covered each of them. In the dream, I knew it was because they were preaching the true gospel aggressively. They called out sin for what it was, addressed lifestyle issues, and challenged the nation's morality. They refused to back down from the truth of God's Word.

I found myself standing at my church's pulpit preaching to a crowd, some of whom I recognized. Most of the people in the back of the church were not listening. Instead, they were asleep or distracted, looking at their watches or playing on their phones. They were not paying attention to the true gospel that I was preaching. Near the altar and the pulpit was a core group of people on their knees praying, listening, and supporting the message.

I observed the screens again and realized that every pastor was addressing the same kind of crowd: distracted multitudes in the pews and the few in the front praying and supporting the message. Without warning, I heard howls outside all the churches. The people at the front turned to look because they sensed something was coming. The people in the back had no reaction to the wolves howling outside.

The wolves then began to scratch on the doors in an attempt to get in. The doors simply opened, and the wolves with normal-looking eyes came in and began walking up and down the pews. I noticed the wolves didn't go near the front. Instead, they climbed into the pews and sat beside those who were sleeping or distracted. Those people absentmindedly stroked the backs of the wolves.

As the wolves listened to the message, they growled and bristled, their eyes turning red. As they rubbed against the people beside them, the people's eyes became red and full of anger. The more the wolves moved, the more they rubbed the people nearby. Very soon, the people began to say things like, "Shut up! Quit preaching. We don't want to hear this! That's not right. That's not fair!" Some were so angry that they left.

The wolves now approached the front, circling the pulpits and biting the preachers' legs. The pastors kept preaching the truth even though it was causing them great pain. Some pastors were even pulled to the ground and mauled by multiple wolves, yet they continued to preach. None of them stood down. Despite being injured and covered in blood, the preachers leaned on their pulpits and preached as hard as possible. Some died at the pulpit, while others limped to their seats after the message ended.

The scene changed to a courtroom. Judges hammered gavels with anger and hostility. They pointed at pastors, demanding that they stop preaching the gospel, condemning certain choices, demonizing abortion, and exhibiting discrimination against people's lifestyles. In the streets, people dragged out pulpits and pulverized them. Others surrounded pastors and Christians to throw things at them and mock them.

I woke up and immediately recognized the primary meaning of the dream. There will be a great uprising of people who have fallen away from serving Christ. They will fight the truth of God's Word and rebel against its Writer, who is the Word of God Himself. This crowd will be those whose love has grown cold as part of the great falling away. The uprising will be hostile and rebellious against those who dare to preach and teach the complete standards, expectations, and mandates of the Word of God.

The Sea Battle
June 26, 2020

I saw the beaches of Normandy, such as Omaha and Utah. Black figures with weapons stood at the old gun turrets. It was as if the Germans had never left. Ships with large sails, some as old as the Niña, Pinta, and Santa Maria, sailed toward the beaches. I was seeing 400 years of colonial and naval ship history. Each ship had people on the top pointing toward the shores and crying, "Get to the beach!" From the hilltops flew cannonballs and missiles from the past 400 years of development. No cannonballs, bullets, or missiles had yet hit the ships, so the onslaught continued. At the bottom of the ships, people were busy praying aggressively for their safety. The closer the ships sailed to the beach, the more the storm of weapons assaulted them. By that time, the vessels that were hit were sinking. The people inside still prayed aggressively and trusted God for victory, but they never made it to shore. Even some iron-clad naval gunships didn't make it.

I realized I was watching 400 years of American history, from the pilgrims to the colonies to the settlers to now. Many trusted God for victories, yet some never made it to the shore.

Simply Dreaming

I saw Hebrews 11, The Hall of Faith, alongside those who hid or got killed. The scene represented centuries of attacks on America. As the ships got closer to the shore, they transformed into modern-looking ships. Those wearing pilgrim clothing now wore the clothing of today. Although each vessel had people praying, some were destroyed and sunk, while others kept sailing. The cannonballs and missiles even evolved into modern weaponry.

This dream revealed that the enemy has always fought against this country's principles, values, and freedoms. As America has aged, the enemy's weapons have become exponentially stronger. Despite constant prayer, the American people have experienced both victories and defeats during the hundreds of years of spiritual warfare. Ultimately, it rains on the just and the unjust.

An Attack on Speaking in Tongues

Late June or Early July 2020

While praying on my church's platform, I had a vision. I saw a lone, rectangular room with no windows and only one door leading outside. On the ground knelt eight people dressed in Middle Eastern-styled white robes with their hands behind their backs. They were men and women of various nationalities. All of them were praying loudly in tongues. I knew this because their languages didn't match their cultures or nationalities.

A dark, hooded figure holding a whip paced behind them. The figure finally stood behind the first man and said, "Stop praying in the Spirit." (This confirmed that the people were indeed praying in tongues.) Instead of stopping, the man prayed louder and with greater intensity. The evil figure began to beat him with the whip. The man continued to pray in the Spirit even louder as the whipping intensified. After a while, the man lay on the floor in pain, mumbling in tongues. The figure beat him into unconsciousness.

The figure changed weapons and stood behind the second person. "Stop praying in the Spirit," he calmly instructed. The woman prayed more intensely, so the beating started. The attack was significant, and the woman whimpered in pain. "I'll stop beating you if you simply stop praying in tongues."

She continued to pray, and her beating grew very aggressive until she curled up in the fetal position. As the figure lifted the weapon once more, the woman finally said, "Okay, I'll stop." He untied her, and she limped out the door.

"The beatings will cease if you simply stop praying in the Spirit," the hooded figure stated again, this time to everyone. Those remaining continued to pray, so the figure lined up behind the next person and prepared to strike.

My vision stopped here. I shared it immediately with the two women in the room with me. Through this vision, I believe God told me that the most effective tool in our spiritual toolbox is to be Spirit-filled and pray aggressively in tongues. The enemy knows this and will do everything in his power to beat this desire out of us through ridicule, physical harm, spiritual threats, attacks, doubt, and persecution. Spirit-filled people must aggressively pursue and develop consistent patterns of praying in tongues, consciously and unconsciously.

The Solemn September Assembly

July 10, 2020

I saw a calendar open to September 2020. A hand tore off the page and placed it on the ground in front of the altar in my church's prayer room, also known as The Secret Place. I could see the altar, the horns on the altar, the pictures on the wall of healing, and Jesus's Second Coming. A voice instructed me, "Stand on September and pray for the Church to have a strong backbone, for corruption to be exposed, and for a great harvest in the coming months." After praying for several minutes, the voice spoke again, "Get help, as you alone are not enough."

I cried out for believers to come to my side and pray with me. As I did, the calendar below me began to get exponentially bigger. I was no longer standing alone on Tuesday, September 1, as several others had joined me. They were praying in every manner and model imaginable: in tongues, loudly, quietly, kneeling, lying prostrate. Together, we cried out that we needed more to come quickly and pray with us.

Moving to the calendar, the hand wrote "A Solemn" in front of September and "Assembly" after it. It ultimately stated,

"A Solemn September Assembly," a clear call to pray during that month. The contours of the calendar moved to fit into the outline of the United States. More people joined the calendar, all praying aggressively as storm clouds blew over the country. There were also fires of revival and fires of opposition to the body of Christ. Astonishing warfare was taking place in the heavens, and saints were becoming weary from the fight. Believers held each other up, stood without division, and fought together in prayer. The battle above was severe, brutal, and intense. The believers were wounded and exhausted because the warfare in the heavens seemed to last forever. But finally, it was over. On the final days of September, the believers were broken and wounded but stood victoriously.

The heavens opened, and I saw the Lord standing with angels behind Him. He said to us,

> Arise, My Bride, arise, My Bride, and prepare to pray. Arise, My Bride, arise, My Bride, and prepare for battle. Arise, My Bride, arise, My Bride, and prepare to see My face. For I am coming soon, and My reward is with Me.

There was a sound like a thousand shofars blowing at once, and I could feel the wind of it on my face.

When I woke, I sensed that the Lord was calling Christians to pray for the entire month of September and that we should expect severe spiritual warfare in response. At the time, I didn't know what would follow September, but I knew that we should expect strenuous spiritual battles. The closer it came to September, the more the Body of Christ needed to prepare spiritually for solid opposition. I didn't declare that the Rapture would happen after these events, but that Jesus is coming soon, and we must be ready.

The Demonic Sleeper Cells
July 25, 2020

A calendar faded from July to August 2020, and the months of August through December became highlighted and bolded. I found myself walking near an abandoned slaughterhouse in my hometown. It was boarded up, surrounded by overgrown weeds and grass, when suddenly it sprang to life. Within the ugly building were demons arming themselves with weapons and preparing for war. It came to me that my hometown was not the only place where these preparations were happening. These demonic "sleeper" cells were awakening all over the country. Minneapolis, Portland, Seattle, and Louisville were just the opening assaults, and these sleeper cells had so much more violence and chaos in store.

The first volley was on ministers and Christian leaders in the area of sexual temptations and accusations. The enemy released the spirits of lust and pornography with a relentless and vicious intent on Christian men across the country. Christian couples in ministry needed to pray together to defend against attacks on

Simply Dreaming

their marriages. Headlines read, "Sudden Nationwide Suicide Spike," which included some Christian leaders. Smoke rose from several outdoor funeral pyres around the nation. Families gathered around each other, sobbing. Angry people demanded the government fix the problems causing mass suicides, such as financial losses, forced evictions, job losses, depression, drug overdoses, and rampant increases in emotional, sexual, and physical abuse. These were all connected to the COVID-19 lockdowns.

Post offices were shut down or only open a few days a week. Customers had to take larger packages to regional offices for shipping. All the small postal trucks not in use were parked in large fields. The streets were heavy with violence. People even threatened government leaders by burning federal buildings to the ground. Elected leaders hid in fear, surrounded by guards. Unemployment rates soared above 50%. More headlines declared, "No Help from Government," which spurred greater violence in Washington, D.C. The crowds became even more heinous in their efforts to get attention. Finally, the White Figure appeared, saying, "Brace yourself, brace yourself, brace yourself," emphasizing the word "brace."

October 2020

August 10, 2020

The calendar month of October 2020 was waving due to a strong, fitful wind. A finger appeared and pointed to the second week of the month, dragging until the end of the third week. Then it prominently pointed to October 31, tapped, and held its position. Immediately, a rock flew out of the sky and landed in a pond. The ripples started small but quickly became vicious waves tossed by an increasing gale.

I saw federally elected officials, state governors, agency leaders, and local radicals with heads like firecrackers with wicks coming out. The federal officials' heads were shaped like M-80 firecrackers, the governors' heads were shaped like Black-Cat firecrackers, and everyone else's heads were shaped like Lady-Finger firecrackers. In the second week of October, all the wicks lit simultaneously. At that moment, everyone's face turned incredibly red. The crowd let out primal screams right before their heads blew up.

Sparks and debris from the explosions ignited many fires. These fires caused protests to step up a notch; at that point, violent protesters oppressed and assaulted bystanders and nonviolent protesters. It was a teaching moment for feeble protestors to understand what the majority expected of them. If the minority was not complicit in protesting "the right way," they were violently attacked and left to die. There was also a clear attack on elderly Americans. I watched small groups knock on doors pretending to be vendors, then assault and rob their aged victims. Some even attempted to get inside nursing facilities to attack bedridden Americans. The mobs were angry at the elderly's constitutional values, faith, and commitment to biblical principles.

The scene changed, and I watched a $100 bill fly like a flag on a flagpole. It was already burning in one corner. As the bill lowered on the pole, some witnesses held their hands over their hearts and cried because their god of money was losing its position of greatness. The bill burned until there was less than a third of it left. Some in the crowd celebrated the death of money with fireworks and loud music; others played Taps.

Inside churches, small groups of people knelt in prayer, wrestling with the spirit of the age. They were doubly protected, having safety bubbles and angels guarding them. These were the faithful core of the Church who had not compromised their values or faith. They were dealing with relentless attacks against them but stayed faithful in prayer. They were not bothered by their small number. There was a narrow gate in the background that they had walked through, like the narrow gate described in Matthew 7:13-14.

In other places, puffed-up pastors and prophets in expensive suits were busy preaching against the idea of coming persecution. Instead, they promised prosperity, health, and good things in store. As they spoke, their words became slurred like drunks. Abruptly, their clothes disappeared, and they tried to cover themselves in vain. The rug was pulled out from under them, and they went flying into the air along with their money. When they landed back on the ground, they bit through their tongues, which flew out of their mouths in pieces and far beyond reach. They couldn't grab their tongues back because they were busy trying to conceal their nakedness. Meanwhile, those praying were still dealing with intense spiritual warfare but were exhibiting strength.

Outside of election venues, I saw signs that read, "Election Is Weeks Away!" Despite this, clowns in business suits were pouring buckets of oil and grease on the ground. Then the clowns danced around while people slipped and slid on the muck. It prevented anyone from getting into the election venues to vote. The clowns tried to distract anyone approaching the venue by juggling and doing sinister and abusive skits. They watched everyone approaching the polls with suspicion and angst.

In the final image, a billboard heralded, "Passover 2021—Big Things Are Coming for The World." This was the first time in my dreams that I saw a reference to the nations, not just America. The White Figure appeared and said to me, "Do not stop bracing, for the storm will not pass until I stop the storm. So, brace, brace, brace yourselves, and don't look back."

The Three Assassination Attempts

August 17, 2020

The calendar month of November 2020 was bent, torn, and dirty. Some trees around me were leafless, while others had a few leaves that were turned as if rain was coming. The sky was a dull gray with extreme cloud cover. A finger appeared and circled November 3 continuously in a clockwise direction but changed to counterclockwise before the images appeared.

I first saw cities on fire and headlines on digital marquees that read, "Trump's Victory Challenged Everywhere." Weary, sleeping protestors lay in the streets, looking incredibly dingy as if they had not slept or showered for weeks. Suddenly, a bell rang loud and clear, and the protestors woke up, salivating like dogs with drops of saliva staining their shirts. Some people were screaming, getting so violent over the election results that they fired weapons randomly in all directions. A man held a sign that read, "The Obvious Winner Is Not So Obvious," and hung his head in shame. The crowd was in a frenzy of hatred, hitting each other in their wrath.

Simply Dreaming

More major cities developed pillars of smoke over them. It looked like the firestorms in California. Meanwhile, in Washington, D.C., I saw crumbled, burned-down businesses and commercial real estate. Headlines declared, "Rebuilding Will Take Time, Gaining Trust Will Take Longer. Government Cannot Do Either in Timely Fashion." Then a treasury official appeared like he was looking at a camera on live TV. With a big smile and open mouth, he winked with his right eye and held it closed.

As the scene changed, Kamala Harris appeared driving a Conestoga wagon led by two mules. Joe Biden rode on the left mule. At Harris' side sat a mechanical box in the upright position that had the power to trigger dynamite. The wind blew the wagon's covering back, revealing several cases of older-styled dynamite and some loose in an open wicker basket. Harris began whipping the mules as well as Biden. The mules started moving, but Biden was oblivious to it. The wagon picked up speed and headed toward its target.

In front of it, Hillary Clinton stood behind President Trump, who was on his knees. She held a Roman Gladius knife to the left side of his neck. She wore what resembled an ugly, unfinished Wilma Flintstone dress and a gaudy ring on her index finger that looked like it had blood on it. A skeleton key hung around her neck and dangled in front of Trump's eyes. The necklace was covered in blood and black mold, which had stained the front of her dress to look like a lightning symbol from the Nazi SS.

As the wagon accelerated, Harris pushed the plunger on the trigger and jumped off as it headed toward Clinton and Trump. Clinton's face was giddy but unbeknownst to her, there was a large animal trap close to her leg. Trump grabbed the key hanging in front of him and pulled it, then punched Clinton's face as it came down. She dropped the knife and stepped into the trap. The President quickly escaped. Three handgun shots rang out, and three different Secret Service agents jumped in front of the bullets to shield Trump as he got into a vehicle and rode to safety. The Secret Service agents wore no sunglasses and surrounded the car with muskets.

Hillary tried to pull her leg out of the trap but could not. The wagon struck her, and the dynamite created an explosion that damaged buildings and created a gigantic hole. The collision threw the mule's carcasses on top of the building's rubble, and the smoke came off them as if the fire had grilled them. Biden lay face down in the middle of the street, wheel tracks scarring him, and a vulture sitting on his head. Harris was crying in disbelief; her tears were the size of quarters.

Then I saw the Church separated with no middle ground left, as sides had been chosen. Fire burned on church altars and above the heads of people in the churches who had been praying. However, question marks sat above some people's heads, and they showed confusion over what they were seeing in the Church and the world. A voice declared, "Those who refuse to get ready will be wanting in the end. So, brace yourself and tell others that I have warned them to brace themselves, for they are about to see even more shocking things."

The Final Warning

August 21, 2020

The White Figure appeared, raised a finger to the sky, and declared, "Ready or not, nation, here it comes. Brace yourself."

The Emergency Shelters

August 24, 2020

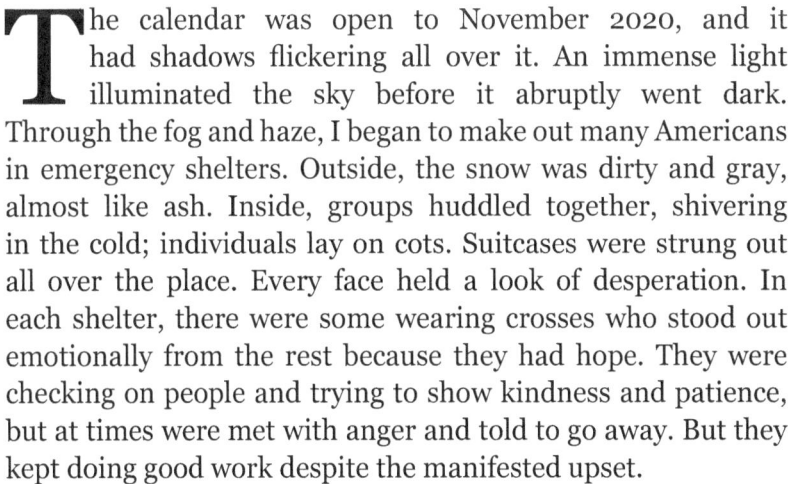

The calendar was open to November 2020, and it had shadows flickering all over it. An immense light illuminated the sky before it abruptly went dark. Through the fog and haze, I began to make out many Americans in emergency shelters. Outside, the snow was dirty and gray, almost like ash. Inside, groups huddled together, shivering in the cold; individuals lay on cots. Suitcases were strung out all over the place. Every face held a look of desperation. In each shelter, there were some wearing crosses who stood out emotionally from the rest because they had hope. They were checking on people and trying to show kindness and patience, but at times were met with anger and told to go away. But they kept doing good work despite the manifested upset.

Some businesses in bigger cities sat shuttered. Gas stations looked like they had simply been abandoned. Headlines read, "Shock and Awe in the U.S." and "U.N. Steps in to Help Host Nation." The country was mostly quiet and fitful, as if it had not yet woken from a bad dream. Overall, the nation felt suspicious and leery of what was coming next. The sun was shining behind the clouds but was not out yet. The White Figure appeared and said to me, "Remain braced as this calm comes before a gathering storm that recovery will have a hard time finding."

The Harsh Winter

August 28, 2020–
September 4, 2020

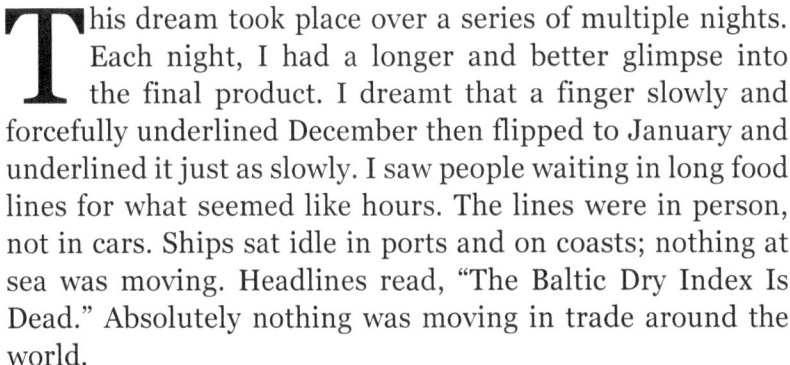

This dream took place over a series of multiple nights. Each night, I had a longer and better glimpse into the final product. I dreamt that a finger slowly and forcefully underlined December then flipped to January and underlined it just as slowly. I saw people waiting in long food lines for what seemed like hours. The lines were in person, not in cars. Ships sat idle in ports and on coasts; nothing at sea was moving. Headlines read, "The Baltic Dry Index Is Dead." Absolutely nothing was moving in trade around the world.

There were no Christmas lights or displays anywhere. A great sadness covered the land, and people seemed dazed and confused. Christians, however, stood out because of their faith and hope in Christ. They appeared like burning charcoal and carried torches wherever they went. Many outsiders rejected their approach, but they kept the faith and didn't back down from telling the lost that they desperately needed Jesus.

Simply Dreaming

It looked like shopping malls had been converted into living shelters, with most businesses shuttered. People still in their homes wore coats and periodically peeked through their closed curtains. Headlines read, "Nationwide Outages Plague Southwest" and "Americans Don't Know Who to Blame for Darkness." Darkness in the Southwest stretched into Canada, and I saw America as lights flickering like a bulb about to go out. Depression walked around like a creature. It wore a mask with a smiley face, but it was choking people, then shoving them to the ground. The vultures from previous dreams were now heavy and had rotting food hanging out of their mouths.

In St. Louis, men with suitcases stood under the Arch. They got into black SUVs and headed both east and west from the Mississippi River. The suitcases looked like nuclear suitcases from the Reagan administration, complete with handcuffs to secure the case to the individual. The men were dressed as businessmen, with heavily tinted sunglasses, carrying copies of the Wall Street Journal under their arms. When their watches went off simultaneously, they picked up the suitcases and got into the vehicles to drive to their destinations.

News headlines read, "Market Crashes, Yields Being Lost" and "Sympathy Declared for Meaning Behind Swastika." The American people had finally lost their resolve to fight due to the emotional overcast of the nation. Yet, Christians remembered what Jesus had said in Matthew 24 about the winter flight, so they kept encouraging one another in the faith. Churches all over the country were keeping their communities secure with a warm glow. The White Figure then rose out of the fires and said, "Brace yourself. Brace, brace, brace yourself on the Word and My promises, and do not rely upon your own strength."

Lady Liberty
September 7, 2021

I admired the Statue of Liberty as she stood proudly in the New York Harbor, lighting the nations in freedom. The sky darkened unexpectedly, and forceful waves began to crash upon the shore with fierce intensity. I noticed men in boats trying to breach the island where Lady Liberty stood, but they couldn't because of the severe storms. Rocks and debris flew at her from all directions with brute force. Lightning hit her torch, flashing brightly. The damage caused her to bleed profusely from her neck and chest.

  Three of the spines on her crown broke off, leaving a jagged edge. Her right hand, which still held the torch, kept dropping to secure the book in her left hand. She struggled to keep her footing and almost slipped several times. A large volley of trash and debris hit her directly in the face, and she stepped back, falling off the pedestal. She got up, still holding the torch, but it was flickering. The declaration in her left hand had cracked, and chips were falling to the ground. Lady Liberty tried to pick up the pieces but would not let go of the torch. Although she was crying, she fought to keep her dignity.

The men in the boats then threw ropes around Lady Liberty's arms and legs and tried to drag her to the ground. They pulled in tandem, and finally, she succumbed, falling to her knees. The men hammered away at the declaration, prying off the letters and numbers. They tried to remove her with cutting tools, and when she wouldn't let go, they cut off her hand. She tried to fight with her other hand, but they had tied it behind her back. The men kept wrapping her in ropes, and she began to yell for help to the point the men took large banners of fabric and covered her face to keep her quiet. They then took an anchor chain, wrapped it around her neck, and asked, "Do you have any last words?"

Her eyes showed no fear and were instead fitful and feisty. She fought back as the boat reversed, pulling her from her pedestal into the harbor. When she was in the water, the boat accelerated to the speed of a ski boat. She twisted back and forth but soon became weary as the boat yanked her along. The banner over her mouth had fallen off, but she said nothing. Eventually, the boat slowed and reversed, running over Lady Liberty, which left her bleeding and bouncing in the harbor. She took a breath and went underwater, coming back up a minute later, then went under again.

When she came up the second time, the boat accelerated and hit her square in the face, circling the area after it hit her. She did not come back up alive. She floated upside down with her torch hand gone and the other arm tied behind her back. There was a thunderous clap and a brilliant lightning strike as the storm raged around the harbor. Something threw pieces of silver at the men, who picked them up feverishly and sped away into the night.

The Tree Grove

September 14, 2020

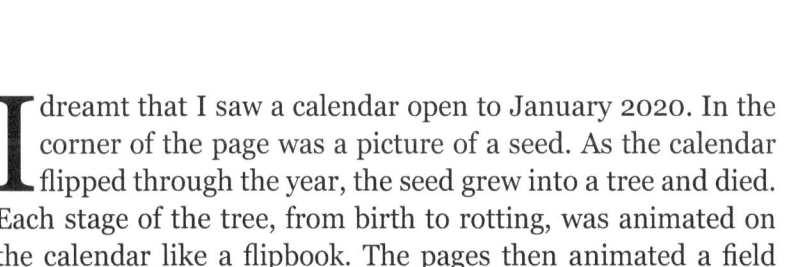

I dreamt that I saw a calendar open to January 2020. In the corner of the page was a picture of a seed. As the calendar flipped through the year, the seed grew into a tree and died. Each stage of the tree, from birth to rotting, was animated on the calendar like a flipbook. The pages then animated a field with bare trees that began to grow leaves, turn colors, and die, leaving a final image of a barren tree field.

    A man dressed like a lumberjack, carrying a large bucket and heavy hammer, trudged up a snowy incline towards the biggest tree in the grove. He had an ancient-looking white beard, and his eyes were constantly closed. He stopped, removed a syrup tap, and hammered it into the tree, but he nailed it at a level higher than his head. He took the bucket, attached it to a hook, and walked away before any movement happened at the tree. At first, a watery pulp appeared, changing to light-colored syrup, then it changed to dark blood. The bucket began to rattle like a fire had lit beneath it, and the blood bubbled and smoked. As it poured out of the tree to the ground like a waterfall, it spelled the words "Guilty as charged."

That same day, I had a vision. An elderly, emaciated woman, weak and malnourished, lay in a hospital bed. The hospital worker beside her bed was the same man with the syrup tap, whom I now recognized as the White Figure. The White Figure (now referred to as the Man) was already an important, recurring figure in my dreams and would become more so with each new dream. As He put down the side rails and lifted her out of bed, the Man clutched the woman tightly to His chest in a loving embrace. His eyes misted over as He gazed lovingly at her.

She tried to open her eyes but didn't have the strength to do so. She could barely whisper, so the Man held her closer to His chest. His lips moved as if He was praying, and He began to blow on her face. He held her hand and squeezed it gently. Her skin was chalk-white, but her hand began to darken as life appeared in it. Her cheeks started turning pink, and her hair became light brown. She then opened her eyes as her body filled out with weight, and her skin returned to its normal complexion.

"Please set me down," she asked.

"Your strength has not returned yet," He replied. "Soon."

"But I am well enough to walk," she said.

The Man knew better. "You need time to rest." The woman started to ask again, but He simply stated, "Do not ask Me again," before gently laying her back in bed and covering her with a blanket.

He walked to the door, looked back at her, and said, "Do not try to walk too soon, or you will limp. You need to be able to stick to the instructions, or you will be ineffective later on. Stay braced and occupy until I come."

The Ten Riders
September 26, 2020

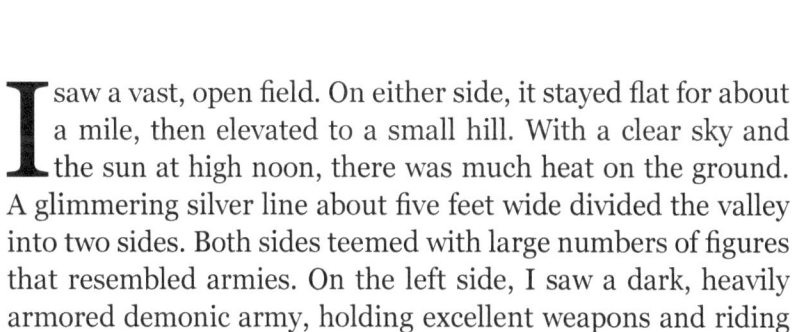

I saw a vast, open field. On either side, it stayed flat for about a mile, then elevated to a small hill. With a clear sky and the sun at high noon, there was much heat on the ground. A glimmering silver line about five feet wide divided the valley into two sides. Both sides teemed with large numbers of figures that resembled armies. On the left side, I saw a dark, heavily armored demonic army, holding excellent weapons and riding red horses. The horses grunted, pranced, and pawed at the ground, so the handlers stroked their necks to calm them. This army was clearly confident and prepared to fight.

The other group was much smaller in number, both mesmerized and shocked by the army in front of them. Of those who had armor, it was shoddy, broken, and ineffective. It was clear this army was disorganized and ill-prepared. Suddenly, from behind them, galloped ten white horses with riders. The men were fully dressed in battle armor, each carrying a large sword that was exceptionally sharp. They rode up quickly behind the small army. The leader of the ten riders addressed the crowd, "It is time to engage. We need everyone for this fight!"

The horsemen rode up and down the front and back of the small army, laying out the victory strategy. Unfortunately, many ignored it and trembled as they gazed at the dark enemy on the other side. The leader raised his sword, and the other horsemen lined up in front of the people. The horsemen yelled, "Charge!" and ran ahead without even one person they had shared the strategy with joining them.

The horsemen charged straight toward the dark army and began clashing swords, fighting in close hand-to-hand combat. The riders kept looking back and asking the others to fight. Instead of helping, some weaker people sat or walked back to the hill. Once at the hill, they began to run upwards but ran out of air about fifty feet from the top. They sat and watched the battle ensue with no energy left, no longer paying any attention to their surroundings. As the battle continued, the riders desperately begged for backup, but no one would cross the line into the battlefield.

A troop of about twenty dark forces, brandishing swords, battle axes, and large clubs, snuck up behind the weak group on the hill. They attacked once they got within a few feet of the oblivious people, beheading five in one swoop. The remainder of the cowardly soldiers dashed toward the battlefield and the line from which they had once retreated. The dark forces made quick work of the group and left their dead bodies in piles on the ground. Those awaiting their deaths yelled to warn the others, who did not hear as they were too busy watching the battle below. The dark forces moved toward the distracted people who had not crossed the line. Upon seeing their attackers, the unprepared army started to panic, looking for weapons and ways to defend themselves.

The ten riders saw the commotion but could not come back to assist because they were still mightily engaged in the battle. The few people remaining tried to get away from their enemies. Without armor and weapons, the demons easily killed them or left them for dead. The part of the dark army that had flanked the retreating army now descended around the ten riders to fight.

The dark forces of the enemy, however, were pushed back, and the men on white horses were successful in the hard-fought battle. But their dead lay on the other side of the battle line, without ever having crossed it. Although the ten leaders on horses kept fighting in strength and anticipation, their fellow soldiers were dead or near death.

The most significant parts of this dream were that only a few were pushing back against the enemy and that it only took a few evil ones to take out the unprepared army. The obvious interpretation is to make sure you are always spiritually prepared. The silver line represents a refined, purified life that is committed and surrendered to Jesus. It requires daily crossing to gain spiritual maturity and win in spiritual warfare.

There is a time that will determine whether we are ready or not, and once that begins, it will be too late to prepare or make up the difference. God is warning us to get ready; if we are not, we will pay the price. Those who are ready will simply be ready, and that is what matters most.

The Data Lines

October 19, 2020–
October 20, 2020

I saw what looked like an atlas with interstate lines all over the nation. The lines were flashing with bits of information going through them. It appeared to be an overloaded network, as some data points were not flashing, and workers in lab coats were trying to fix them. A few areas were heating up, and the workers shared concerns that the circuits would fry if they couldn't slow down the overloaded system. Bright flashes and smoke suddenly appeared from the data points of bigger cities from the west coast to the Mississippi River. The workers feverishly attempted to fix the problem but could not get the system back online. Their short-term solution was to reroute the areas close to the big cities, which settled those small areas but left the bigger cities smoking.

A countdown clock started backward from ten, and when it reached one, everything got worse. The points east of the Mississippi River began to flash, their cities blew up in smoke, and the circuits fried. When the flashes reached Philadelphia, the network line, now flashing red, moved to the Liberty Bell.

The line went directly underneath the bell and began to pulse. It looked like a red firehouse as it flashed and built pressure, and when it blew, it sent the Liberty Bell into the air, where it was cut entirely in half. When it landed, both sides fell onto their rounded exterior edge and rolled for a while until they both stopped rocking and began to melt.

The data lines ravenously raced toward Washington, D.C. The city had octopus arms that were fighting to disconnect the data lines from entering. One line kept flashing and pulsing, even though people in suits and ties were trying to pull its connections out of the Capitol Building. When the line finally blew up, the building cracked in half, and a looming smoke cloud appeared that spelled "Discovery." People ran away, but not from the explosion; they ran from the word in the sky.

In the Capitol's rotunda sat a closed casket. A sign read, "Inside Lies Joe Biden, Democratic Candidate for the Office of the President." A calendar hanging above his casket had the date December 17, 2020, circled. Biden's wife and one of his sons were in the room looking at their feet. Many members of Congress and senators from both parties were present, looking at the floor and shaking violently. Their shoes had been piled in the doorway when they walked in, so they were barefoot.

A prominent senator stood, demanding, "I want to see the body!"

The Sergeant at Arms rushed to the casket with several Marines and said, "There will be no viewing of the body today or ever again."

The senator sat down and collected himself, then walked to the shoe piles. He dug until he found his own, put them on, and sprinted out the door. Smoke was still rising as he ran towards the White House with clenched fists and curses on his lips. He stopped for a moment near the Washington Monument and looked back to see twenty to twenty-five others following, holding their shoes in their hands as they walked. "Hurry!"

he yelled, but they continued their slow and steady pace. He sneered at them and began sprinting again toward the White House.

I then saw the Man standing where presidents give the State of the Union Address. He tapped the microphone three times and loudly stated, "A house divided against itself *shall* not stand." He pushed the microphone down and walked to the door at the rear of the room. On the wall were several light switches, all of which He turned off.

Hold Your Breath

October 26, 2020–
October 27, 2020

It was daytime across America, and people were doing various things, like shopping, attending church, visiting banks, and watching games at ballparks. No one wore masks or was concerned about what was happening. People were acting as if 2020 wasn't bad at all. Then suddenly, many people started looking around as if they had heard something. Some took a deep breath as if they were about to jump into water. They were not straining, just calmly watching the landscape before them. Others, however, had not heard anything and kept doing what they were doing, completely unaware of anyone holding their breath.

Waves of water suddenly swept over the mountains that encircled the whole country. It was as if America was a pool about to be filled, but only those holding their breath knew what was happening. Those holding their breath were not fearful at all. They were calm, some with their family at their sides, standing squarely in place. The others, however, saw the water and began to panic, scream, and run, yet they had no place to go. They cursed the sky and God as the water reached their knees. There were no buildings to run to, just open fields.

There were two distinct groups: those holding their breath and those who had not even thought to try. One group was caught off guard and running, while the other was calm. The Man walked out of the group, which collectively held its breath. He held up two fingers on His right hand and said to me, "Stay braced, but don't breathe just yet."

Benjamin Franklin
November 16, 2020

Benjamin Franklin was flying a kite during a stormy night. Upon closer inspection, I saw that his kite was an American flag that had an oily, greasy sheen. A globe and chain were attached to the end of the kite like a keychain. Franklin held the kite steady in the rain and watched the lightning around him with wide-open eyes. Unexpectedly, a Hand appeared out of Heaven, which roughly grabbed the flag and squeezed it tight. The Hand released oil onto the globe before the globe fell to the Earth and was illuminated by lightning. The Hand kept squeezing and rolling back and forth as if it were sifting something inside.

The rain ceased, and the Hand opened to reveal several large diamonds and large chunks of coal. There was so much trash, however, that it was difficult to see the diamonds. God then blew into His palm, releasing the trash while the diamonds and coal remained. He lowered His hand to the ground and rolled out the items. The diamonds were the size of vehicles, and the coals were the size of boulders. Each item lay in beautiful, green, luscious grass. The diamonds were shining with quality brilliance; despite being squeezed, the coals had no shimmer of glory.

Franklin admired the scene before him and solemnly said, "I guess we are no longer a republic."

God's voice responded, "No, it's Mine now, as is the whole Earth."

"Where is the globe that was attached to the flag?" Franklin asked.

"It's still being pressured for now but will be released in good time," replied the Father. "Keep your glasses on, your eyes sharp, and stay committed to the captain."

Abraham Lincoln's Assassination

November 9, 2020

Abraham Lincoln stood at the Lincoln Memorial with his right hand up as Uncle Sam addressed him. Several spotlights were aimed at his head, which bathed him in overwhelming light. It looked like Abraham Lincoln had been assaulted. He had marks on his face, a sling over his left arm, and a bandage around his left hand with bloodstains on the palm. Although he kept a stern face, Lincoln was obviously in pain from whatever had happened. Close by, his granite seat was stacked high with items that together formed a pyramid. His brown leather Bible was on the bottom, which was the largest and thickest book of all, followed by his law books and tall hat.

Uncle Sam asked Lincoln, "Do you solemnly swear that you will tell the truth, the whole truth, and nothing but the truth, so help you God?"

"That is all you will get from me on this day," Lincoln replied.

Uncle Sam walked backward, stepped onto a platform, and removed his patriotic hat. "I am sorry," he whispered to Lincoln. Uncle Sam shifted his eyes right, left, and right again as if someone acknowledged him.

"Get it over already!" a voice shouted.

Someone pulled a black curtain along a fifty-foot piece of rope to create a backdrop between two tattered American flags. The judge found his place on center stage while Lincoln remained standing. Uncle Sam cleared his throat three times and said, "Hear ye, hear ye. The accused before you is here to admit his crimes publicly and will do so voluntarily. How do you plead, Mr. Lincoln?"

President Lincoln never blinked, but he swallowed hard. "I won't."

Uncle Sam winked at Lincoln and asked again, grimacing to get his attention. "I won't," Lincoln insisted.

Uncle Sam looked beyond the curtain behind him, then looked back wearily. "Mr. Lincoln, you must make a plea."

"Well, then give me a trial by jury after I do," he replied, simply looking straight ahead and saying nothing further.

Two men walked up behind Uncle Sam, each to a different ear, and whispered something. He grimaced and dropped his head as the two men disappeared behind the curtain. Uncle Sam stood before Lincoln and the watching crowd. The crowd was aggressive and mean-spirited, holding signs and torches. After looking both to his right and left, then at the two men who had stood behind Uncle Sam, Lincoln straightened his posture and closed his eyes slowly. Federally elected and federally appointed officials, governors, and judges watched him closely.

With tears running down his cheeks, Uncle Sam approached Lincoln and whispered, "Mr. Lincoln, you have been found guilty by those in power and are sentenced to death by hanging."

"As the former President of this Union, I deserve to know

what I am accused of in the first place. I am an attorney, and I know what the law says."

With great struggle, Uncle Sam responded, "We do not recognize the law of man or the law of God, and simply find you worthy of death. Your time is over, and a new dawn awaits those who will dwell on this Earth."

The men standing behind Uncle Sam came forward, put a noose around Lincoln's neck, and tightened it. They pushed Uncle Sam forward while they threw the end of the rope over the marble brace in the memorial. The men handed Uncle Sam the end of the rope and saluted him. He held the rope in his hands for a long time and wept. Finally, he faced Lincoln and cried, "I am sorry, Mr. President."

At this statement, the men pounded Uncle Sam's head and neck until bruising appeared and demanded, "You will address him as Mr. Lincoln, nothing more."

Uncle Sam looked at the men and declared, "You can hang me next for what I have allowed you to do to my conscience." Then he started pulling the rope. President Lincoln stood quietly. As he felt the tautness of the rope, he reached toward his chair in a fight to grab his Bible and law books. Uncle Sam strained to pull because of the movement. Lincoln's fingers kept slipping off the binding of the books. When he finally got a hold of them, his feet lifted from the floor, and the books fell.

Lincoln's eyes displayed compassion toward the elected and appointed men in front of him, but Uncle Sam only looked at the floor. Lincoln finally stopped fighting back after his Bible slipped from his hands. Now he swung slowly. "You can drop him now," said one of the judges.

Uncle Sam slowly and respectfully dropped Lincoln onto the floor. He looked back at the men and said, "I hope you get what you deserve for this," then held his chest and dropped to the floor. Uncle Sam was dead within seconds, with his eyes wide open. The crowd began to scatter, including the elected and appointed men.

At that moment, the Man appeared. He knelt beside President Lincoln and said, "They didn't have any idea what they were doing, and now the nation needs to brace itself for what it deserves." He walked to Uncle Sam, closed his eyes tenderly, tapped his heart three times, and said, "Rest in peace, Uncle Sam. Sorry you had to see the ship go down." He looked right at me and said, "Nation, brace yourself for fire and ice, and don't forget to anchor your soul."

The Church and the State

December 19, 2020–
December 23, 2020

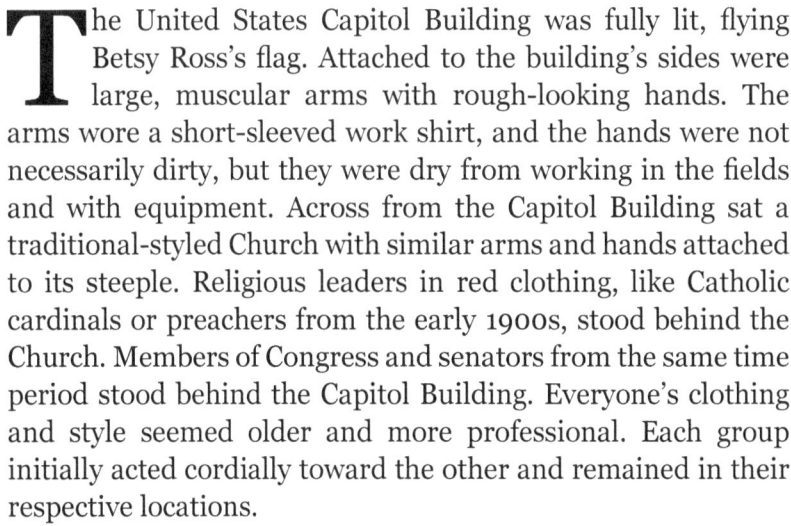

The United States Capitol Building was fully lit, flying Betsy Ross's flag. Attached to the building's sides were large, muscular arms with rough-looking hands. The arms wore a short-sleeved work shirt, and the hands were not necessarily dirty, but they were dry from working in the fields and with equipment. Across from the Capitol Building sat a traditional-styled Church with similar arms and hands attached to its steeple. Religious leaders in red clothing, like Catholic cardinals or preachers from the early 1900s, stood behind the Church. Members of Congress and senators from the same time period stood behind the Capitol Building. Everyone's clothing and style seemed older and more professional. Each group initially acted cordially toward the other and remained in their respective locations.

The clouds drifting in the sky above seemed to pick up speed, which reminded me of the time element sequence in H.G. Wells' *The Time Machine*. When the scene slowed down, the Capitol Building's arms wore long sleeves with expensive cufflinks, and its hands were now soft and manicured. The building was brightly lit, well-maintained, and polished. The Church's muscled arms had not changed, and it still had dry, cracked hands from constant work. The Capitol Building put its hands together, popped its knuckles, and pointed at the Church in accusation. The Church's now bloody hands kept moving forward and working. The Capitol's hands raised to stop the Church from moving forward, and the Church stopped in its tracks. The Church's hands moved to explain that they needed to get past the Capitol Building, but it stood in the way. The Church tried to make its way through politely, but the Capitol pushed the Church hard, knocking it down. The Church stayed down for a few minutes only to stand back up and get knocked down again.

This scene repeated several times, with the Church showing caution but not backing down. The Church stood its ground each time, getting firmer in its approach. The people behind the Church were timid, but the people behind the Capitol Building were intimidating, with folded arms and grimaces on their faces. The Church finally popped its knuckles, set its face beyond the Capitol, and tried to walk by, stating, "We need to get by, and we are going to do it right, but we must be allowed to pass."

The Capitol Building responded, "Not on our watch." It grabbed the Church by the throat and pushed it away, but now the Church fought back. The Church leaned into the Capitol, put its foot back in place, and both buildings strained against each other. As they pushed and contended together, the Capitol slipped a seed into the Church's back pocket. At the same time, some standing behind the Church moved to stand behind the Capitol Building.

"Stand down!" roared the Capitol.

"We won't!" cried the Church.

During their standoff, a large, thorny vine grew out of the Church's back pocket and wrapped around its neck. Upon seeing this, the Capitol finally let go of the Church and let it walk forward. The vine's red flowers now bit the Church as the vine wrapped around its legs. The vine kept growing, driving into the Church's mouth and down its throat until it surrounded the Church's heart.

The Capitol was no longer concerned about the Church's struggle. The Church's right hand had turned white, and its left hand was red from the vine's flowers that were tangled in its fingers. The vine's leaves looked like flags, all red with unusual symbols on them. The Church started pulling the vine out of its throat with its left hand, but its right hand slapped it away. The two hands began to fight each other, one trying to protect the vine and the other trying to strip it away. As the struggle continued, the Capitol periodically looked at the Church to assess its strength but kept busy handing out money, signing bills, and shaking hands with business leaders from many nations.

The Church began to shake violently like it was having a grand-mal seizure. Its chest then split open to reveal a heart that had been almost squeezed to death by the vine. The Church's white hand grabbed a knife and pierced the root around the heart, which caused the vine to wither. The red hand made a fist, punched the steeple, and tried to grab the white hand, but its strength faded. The white hand pulled the root from its heart, buttoned its shirt, and fell to its knees. "Please forgive me for allowing the red root to grow in my pocket," the Church prayed.

The Man appeared and embraced the Church. He pointed to the Capitol Building and said, "You never wanted the Church to succeed, but the gates of Hell will not stop her. And those who have seen the root will prune the vine and cut off the poisonous part." He turned to the Church and said, "Be about My Father's business. Stay pure and fear not the State, for they know not what they do."

Simply Dreaming

The Church trudged past the Capitol but began running after passing it by a few yards. Both of its hands were now white, and laying at the Capitol's feet was the root of the seed it had planted in the Church's back pocket. The Man spoke clearly, "Stay braced, stay focused, and stay on task, for I am coming soon."

The Birds and the Maul

January 1, 2021–
January 4, 2021

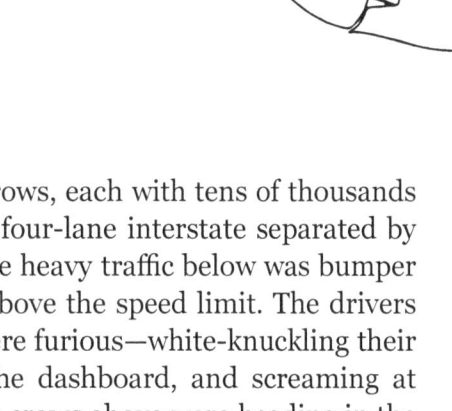

Two distinct flocks of crows, each with tens of thousands of birds, flew above a four-lane interstate separated by a median. Although the heavy traffic below was bumper to bumper, everyone drove above the speed limit. The drivers on both sides of the traffic were furious—white-knuckling their steering wheels, pounding the dashboard, and screaming at other drivers. Meanwhile, the crows above were heading in the same direction as the traffic in the right lanes, which was to a tunnel many miles ahead. The flocks kept bumping into each other, and each time, a few birds would fall to the ground and never get back up. The two flocks of crows appeared to be flying into each other intentionally to cause damage.

As the crows soared, little flashes of lightning popped sporadically in the distance. After each strike, a leader bird from each side left the group, taking fifty to a hundred birds along as it chased the flashes. The leader crows weaved quickly and dangerously through oncoming traffic, and their followers grew

Simply Dreaming

dizzy. One lead bird hazardously led its followers towards a semi-truck and the other towards the cement wall of an overpass. At the very last second, each leader bird suddenly flew straight up away from the impending danger, but their followers were not quick enough to react, hitting the objects and dying at once.

The leaders then rejoined the main groups and, with each flash of lightning, led more groups of crows to their death. The birds in the main groups continued flying toward the tunnel that carried all four lanes of traffic. The tunnel had large American flags hanging above it, but each flag was dirty, ragged, and tattered. The flags were connected with red and white fabric that together looked like candy canes. The wind violently blew the flags and ripped them.

The Man appeared on top of the flags. He wore a medieval metal helmet and chainmail and carried a giant sword the size of a Scottish Claymore at His side. He held a metal spike as tall as Himself and a metal maul (a long-handled hammer with a spike on one end) that looked like a medieval mace. As the birds approached the tunnel, the Man, who now looked like He was ten feet tall, lifted the maul into the air. The maul changed into an anvil on a wooden handle, and blood dripped down the handle onto His hands.

The traffic disappeared, and the road transformed into a runway. Both groups of crows merged and took on the shape of a stealth bomber as they sped toward the ever-growing tunnel. Blind people wearing masks and using white canes filled the tunnel's dark hole. As the birds flew closer to the tunnel, the Man began driving His spike into the ground above the tunnel's entrance. The ground trembled and cracked open; air screamed as it rushed to the surface. He kept pounding the spike until the tunnel began to collapse. The ground shook like an earthquake. He took off his helmet and feverishly continued to hit the spike as the ground shook more and the ceiling tunnel began to collapse on the people below.

Because the people were blind, they were unaware of the rocks falling on them. They continued to meander aimlessly in the tunnel, falling to the ground like they were dead after being battered by the debris. The crows entered the tunnel right as it collapsed, leaving them crushed flat and buried under the rubble. The flags above had burned to ash, and the wind blew the residue into the air.

Then, out of the destruction came the Man carrying the maul in His hands. He placed the helmet back on His head and the maul on the ground. "Justice for all is coming but will not be seen by the many who needed it desperately," He announced. "Bracing is required to stay the course, but it will be a course of consequence." The ground began to shake, and men, none of whom were soldiers, started taking up arms and lining up, ready to fight. As reveille sounded, the men marched forward with intent in their eyes.

The Plumb Line

January 9, 2021–
January 11, 2021

I stood under a bright, sunny sky with no clouds. From my vantage point, I could see the traditional skyline of New York City and the Empire State Building. The Man walked at a steady pace down the street. He wore a first-century Jewish robe and a prayer shawl over His head. The people who walked by Him didn't notice He was carrying a rope that hung to the ground. A large stone tablet like that of the Ten Commandments was attached to the rope's end. The rope remained tight, so the tablet never swung while He walked.

I walked beside Him, paying careful attention to the rope and the stone. I finally asked Him, "Why do the rope and stone not move or wobble as You walk?"

"My plumb line never moves," He replied.

"Where are we going?" I wondered.

"To do My business," He answered.

We passed the sign for Wall Street and continued walking. Several feet past the sign, He stopped and peered into the

Simply Dreaming

distance at a taller building, then held up the rope and measured the plumb line against it. I could see that the building was obviously tilted away from the plumb line. The Man pushed the building with both hands, and it began to shake back and forth, still rocking even after He removed His hands. Suddenly, the windows opened, and I watched as furniture and people fell out and hit the ground. Files, folders, and currency of all kinds (not just American) fell out of the windows. Before they hit the ground, a violent wind swept them into the air, preventing them from hitting the pavement. The people on the ground were bruised and struggling to walk. An oily pitch-like tar covered their suits, which glued them down. They could move, but not effectively.

The Man told me to follow Him, so I did. As I followed, I could see the Capitol Building on the horizon. It was twisted in much the same way as the building on Wall Street. We walked toward it briskly, saying nothing to each other. Once we stood at the bottom of the Capitol's steps, the Man held up the rope. He raised His right foot high in the air, took off His sandal, and brought His foot down roughly on the first step.

The Capitol began to rock back and forth, and soon people, documents, and nameplates were falling out of the windows and doors. People screamed in pain as they landed roughly on their knees, yet they couldn't get up because they were covered in sticky purple syrup thick as molasses. When they did get up, they'd slip and get covered in the mess. The people remained silent but angrily shook their fists at the Man until they eventually dropped their heads to hide their faces. Half of them wept, and the other half lay in a fetal position and groaned.

"Follow me," He instructed me.

By this time, the sun had set. We approached a church with modern architecture and a large, green neon cross on the roof. The glowing cross seemed to be on a preset cycle, glowing brighter from green to white, then fading repeatedly. The Man walked up to the church, then took off His outer robe and prayer shawl. He grew until He was larger than the church, placed both His hands on it, and lifted it into the air. "I warned them," He told me. He shook the church aggressively and violently until the cross's light went out, the windows shattered, and the outer walls began to tear apart from each other. He slammed the church down, and the front doors broke off their hinges.

People stumbled out of the church and ran away as fast as they could. They threw their Bibles to the ground and didn't even look back at us. It became clear that the people were pastors, and they were hiding their identities as they ran. Many simply shook their heads and denied knowing Jesus as they walked by a crowd who watched them. I stepped inside the church to look. It was incredibly damaged, as pews were turned over and broken, lights hung from the damaged ceiling, and a chandelier dangled close to the floor from an electrical wire. The oak pulpit was intact but chipped and leaning.

At the front of the church, hundreds of people were tied to the altar with ropes and chains. They clutched their Bibles so tightly that their handprints left imprints on the covers. Although they looked weak and weary, their faces were joyful. Some were dead, having been hit by debris from the shaking. Those still alive shed tears for the fallen but got up and began to clean the area.

The Man walked in, assessed the scene, and declared, "You took warning and were good to do so. Your obedience has been noted, and there will be fruit both here and in Heaven. Though shaken and broken, you will arise, My Bride, and work until I come."

Biden's Inauguration
January 10, 2021

I stood at the bottom of the ceremonial area at the Capitol Building where presidents are inaugurated. Everyone present wore blue jackets or dresses, and blue confetti flew everywhere. Joe Biden was directed to stand by the Chief Justice, and he pushed a walker to do so, falling twice along the way. Each time he fell, everyone looked away without helping him get back up. Biden grew angry but kept smiling despite his pain.

When Biden finally reached the stands, Justice Roberts said, "Raise your right hand." But instead, Biden raised his left hand and waved to the crowd. Justice Roberts began reading, "Repeat after me. I, Joseph Robinette Biden, do solemnly swear."

"Robin and I solemnly swear," he stammered, stuttering more as he noticed everyone on the platform glancing at their watches.

"Do you need me to repeat the phrase?" the judge asked.

"I am not a stupid man, Judge," Biden insisted. "I, senator-elect Biden, do hereby—"

Without warning, a shot rang out, and blood appeared on Biden's shirt. "They got me right in the heart!" he cried, slamming his hand against his chest theatrically. He fell backward, hit his head hard on the floor, shut his eyes, and smiled.

The crowd matter-of-factly cleared the platform. There was no screaming or panicking over Biden's "death." Justice Roberts removed his black robe, covered the body, took a bulging white envelope from his chest pocket, and placed it in Biden's left hand. Although Biden's body was under the robe, his right hand reached out from beneath the robe to shake the judge's hand.

The judge had started to move away when he was shot from behind. He fell to his knees as a pool of blood formed on his chest. Men wearing suits and ear monitors appeared and pulled away the bodies. As the men dragged him, Biden spoke from under the robe, "Hey man, I may be old, but please treat me with kid gloves because you're hurting me." The guards then kicked him and pulled him up the stairs.

They Don't Hate Me; They Hate You

January 26, 2021

I stood with a woman who was in labor. The baby was born covered in blood, and the mother passed away from complications. A nurse wrapped the baby in a white receiving blanket and laid him on the bed. Although the blood soaked through the blanket, I intuitively knew the baby would live.

Hundreds of cribs lined the hospital nursery, each holding a sleeping or crying baby. Only twelve to fifteen nurses were on duty, and they were stressed as they scurried around trying to take care of the babies. Some nurses held two or three babies at a time and struggled to feed them as the babies wailed. The Man stood in the room wearing a white coat; He was clearly the doctor. He told me, "The harvest is full, but not enough are helping."

The scene changed to Washington, D.C, and two F-16s flew in a wide circle around the city's boundaries. They would circle and then fly towards each other, but not in the same line, then go

Simply Dreaming

back to circling but in opposite directions. The jets had sensor-like equipment on their bellies and missiles under each wing. Their pilots were closely watching the airspace around them.

Inside the Capitol Building, the chamber had furnaces without wood or fire. Instead, the furnaces had suction devices like a tube with air rushing to the outside of the building. The members of Congress and senators were busy shoving $100 bills into the furnaces, which were then sucked through the pipes and tossed by the wind. People outside in heavy winter coats jumped and reached for the money but couldn't grab it, as it was far above them. Even people on the top of the Capitol Building couldn't catch the cash with their nets as it flew past.

Then, I saw thirty congressmen and senators barricaded in the middle of the Capitol's balcony. Some of them had signs of recent beatings. A non-military police unit surrounded them with rifles, body armor, helmets, and covered faces, showing extreme aggression toward the elected officials.

One senator stood and yelled, "I demand to know why we are being held here like prisoners!"

In response, an officer hit the senator in the face with the butt of his rifle. "Stop asking questions!" he demanded.

The scene quickly changed to the floor where President Trump stood to address the State of the Union. Trump was in handcuffs, one ear bleeding bright red, the other bruised black and blue. His eyes were bloodshot, and he appeared to be barely standing on his own. The Sergeant at Arms stood directly behind him, holding him up and whispering into his ear. Occasionally he would squeeze the President's right arm, making the President wince and almost drop to his knees. President Trump suddenly pushed himself forward out of the Sergeant's grip and said, "It's not me they hate; it's you." He then rushed out the door.

A congressman approached the podium and hit the gavel so severely that it broke the gavel and dented the table. "Let's get the rest of them because it's our house now," he declared. He peered into the balcony at those held by the police and said, "Put them with the rest."

The Man, no longer dressed like a doctor, stood up in the middle of the room and shouted, "I never said to stop bracing." He then helped those beaten leaders to their feet and walked with them through the doors in the back of the balcony. He looked back as He walked through the door and said, "Stay braced for His name's sake."

When I awoke, I understood that the scene in Washington, D.C., and the Capitol Building shows how political persecution of the Church will become a reality. But the Lord will walk through with us and help us "stay braced for His name's sake."

The Bunker
February 8, 2021

I saw Washington, D.C.'s skyline and an overview of the White House. Its lights were out, and no official business was taking place in the building. A phone inside kept ringing, but there was no one to answer it. Every computer was off, and electronic devices sat on desks hooked up to their chargers, glowing green to indicate their batteries were full. The analog wall clocks were frozen at different times, while the digital clocks had been unplugged. The rooms were clean, but the Oval Office was quite dusty. A grandfather clock sat in front of the room's closed curtains, but its pendulum was not moving. On the wall hung a red and white sign edged with gold barbed wire that seemed to glow. It stated, "Business as Usual Is Over for Everyone."

    I was transported to a bunker that I sensed was below the White House. The bunker had a large sign on the wall with the White House's symbol. In the middle of the floor sat a conference table that held sixteen men dressed in military uniforms, dark suits, and black-tinted sunglasses. Several of the military men wore their medals and ranks. They were busy looking at thick folders in front of them, which read "Top-Secret Classification" and "The American Solution."

One man stood and saluted the others individually. He addressed them, "Today, we leap off the mountain and fly towards a new beginning. Many, though not us, will hit the precipice moments later, but we will not even have to look back or look down as we have better places to go." All the men nodded and hit the table with their fists. "Gentleman, please report," the man instructed.

A man wearing a suit stood and said, "Three events are planned, but if the first one hits hard enough, the other two will not be needed. Our target groups will be easily identified in the events, and the rest of America will demand their arrests and imprisonments immediately, perhaps even their executions."

The first speaker stood again, looked at the man wearing the darkest sunglasses, and asked, "What do you have to offer?"

The gentleman stood and replied, "Hoover will be proud, sir, and our list is pristine. Better than he ever was."

He sat down, and the first speaker said, "All in favor?"

They all hit their fists on the table and shouted, "Favor!"

Back in the Oval Office, the curtains were now open to a gray, overcast day with sprinkling rain. The grandfather clock's pendulum moved so fast that the clock rattled. Four soldiers walked into the room, two wearing American uniforms and two wearing blue military uniforms. All four had black head coverings that hid their faces. They saluted the empty desk and started shooting up the room with handguns. A soldier in a blue uniform removed the barbed wire from the sign and placed it on the Resolute Desk with a handwritten note that said, "My office is surrounded."

The scene changed to the outside of the White House, which was surrounded by military and concertina wire. The Man stepped out from the Rose Garden, saying, "Bracing will save many but will also speak to many. They will hunt you, and when you stand before the haters, I will prompt your words to convict their hearts. It has started, and darkness is in the winds, so brace and speak. And don't stop speaking."

The Mud

February 18, 2021–
February 20, 2021

I saw a snowy, icy landscape so thick with fog that I couldn't see through it. As the fog cleared, I made out the outline of southern coastal states from Texas to Florida and buildings resembling churches in each state. Each church had smoke coming out of it, and believers inside prayed loudly and earnestly. The believers cried many tears and wailed as they interceded for their unsaved loved ones. They repented and confessed the nation's sins as well as their own. They asked God's forgiveness for being inadequate witnesses, for being anchored to sins they knew were wrong, and for holding onto their chains and letting their sin ruin their relationship with Him.

As they prayed, my vantage point shifted, and I was above the Earth, looking down at those states. The louder and more aggressively the people prayed in each church, the quicker the snow and ice melted away from the buildings. As the snow disappeared, however, it left behind a gray mud that smelled of death and decay. There was very little green vegetation and no leaves on the trees. The ground was dead and exposed. The believers walked out of the churches and began holding their noses, asking God why He had not answered their prayers to bring restoration to the land.

The heavens opened, and the voice of God answered, "Work with the mud you have been given." Some immediately complained of the hours they had been praying, expecting a better return for their prayers. The voice of God repeated firmly, "Work with the mud you have been given."

A cloud appeared, heading directly over the muddiest ground. While some believers began to follow it, others walked away in disappointment. Those who walked away passed the churches, leaving their prayer guides and Bibles behind, saying, "We will find better ground and a god that will honor our prayers." The ones who followed the cloud were in the mud up to their knees and struggling to move, but they gritted their teeth and pushed forward. Suddenly, the howling of wolves erupted, and the mud walkers stopped to listen, but only for a moment. They didn't give in to their fears and kept chasing the cloud.

Like an ambush, hundreds of black wolves pushed through the mud to get close to the believers. They snarled and tried to bite the believers but were seemingly held back at the last moment. At times, the wolves were just inches from the people's faces, but the people remained focused on following the cloud. They looked up as a group to stay steady on the path. The sky was clear, but the ground was muddy and ashen gray. The sunlit sky revealed the depth of the mud and the sweat of the people trudging through it.

The scene changed, and I saw the entire United States. Each state had a group of people trudging through the mud toward the cloud at the very center of the nation. The cloud was now stationary, but everyone was focused, pushing through the mud and avoiding the wolves along the way. The closer they got to the cloud, the braver the wolves got, now making contact

The Mud

when they bit, leaving marks on the believers. Yet, the people continued.

The wolves' innumerable paw prints littered the landscape, and their eyes began to glow bright red with intensity. As the wind picked up, people outside the mud, wearing masks of skulls, witches, and demons, provoked the wolves to attack the believers. The masked people screamed curses and blasphemous words at the believers in the mud, calling them haters and dividers. Although there was no mob leader, some threw rocks and sticks like arrows at those trudging through mud.

The believers kept pushing toward the cloud, although they were covered head to toe in grime. The stronger ones pulled the weaker ones by hand or carried them on their backs. Although most had looked at the solid ground with distress, they refused to quit the journey. A few paused, however, to consider getting out of the mud, while others left entirely, helped by those wearing masks. Once out of the mud, those wearing masks gave their new companions masks of their own, who began to taunt those still slogging along toward the cloud. "The mud is not God's plan! He has deceived you, and yet you follow without thinking for yourselves," they jeered.

The Man then appeared in a white robe with angels all around Him. He held a scepter in His right hand. He spread His arms and spoke powerfully,

> My ways are not your ways. Your spiritual legs will be strengthened through agony, and your witness will offend the naïve and those who have no fear of Me. Bracing gives way to fire, and those braced must remain on the path. My command is to come out from among them, separate yourself, as the chaff is about to burn, and the smoke will fill the skies.

The sky filled with green lightning and claps of thunder for a long time. Blinding flashes of light illuminated the entire country so intensely that even the shadows disappeared. The wolves hid their faces in the earth, and the people harassing the

Simply Dreaming

believers hid their faces in shame. The Man rose to the sky and thrust the scepter towards the Earth, shouting, "I am coming soon, and My reward is with Me. Stay faithful until I come."

Air Force One
March 1, 2021

I saw Air Force One flying recklessly in the sky. It was alternatively speeding up and slowing down, and its right wing shook like it was loose or coming apart. There were no protective fighter pilots anywhere in sight. The aircraft began to take on even riskier flying, and I found myself inside the cabin, looking at the cockpit. President Biden was flying the plane, pushing buttons, and smiling when it made noises. He pulled handles and moved things while the co-pilot stared out the window ignoring him.

Biden began to talk to himself and got up to look out the window, commenting on how blue the sky was and how far the ground was below. He then sat back down and fell asleep. His co-pilot watched him nod off and then proceeded to do the same, snoring within a few minutes. Eventually, a message from the cockpit stated, "Autopilot has been engaged, but do not expect a smooth ride even once we land."

The Elder
March 8, 2021

President Biden was struggling to stand up from his Resolute Desk. Vice President Harris, who stood behind him, came forward to help him stand, revealing a walker in front of his desk chair. Biden looked incredibly frail as he grabbed the walker's handles. He tried to take a step but couldn't get his legs to move. Harris got behind him and pushed his feet with hers while she helped him balance enough to stand with the walker.

"Slow down, please; I can't go that fast," he told her. When he got to a table in the office, he stopped and patted a bust of Robert Kennedy, saying, "Sorry they got you, Bobby, but they had to, you know, because you knew too much."

"Sir, we need to get you to your room, so keep moving," Harris said.

"Please don't take me there," Biden replied. "I hate it there, and I don't like the feel of the air in that room."

Harris kept pushing him anyway, to the point that she almost knocked him over the walker. She pressed a button on her jacket and whispered, "I need an agent immediately to assist with The Elder."

Simply Dreaming

Two Secret Service agents walked in, and one loaded Biden onto the other's back, who carried him through the door into an elevator. The other agent stood with his back to the elevator doors as they began to close. He then hit his microphone and said, "Elder secured and heading downstairs. Oval Office stable, and my eyes are on the door. What you do now, do it quickly."

The Man appeared in an expensive suit. He walked from the elevator to the Oval Office and stood behind the Resolute Desk. He upturned it, which caused two drawers to open and papers to float toward the ground. The Man pushed the desk towards the front of the room, and the empty floor revealed bloodstains in front of the presidential chair.

"Don't let the suit fool you or the office either," He told me. "What's under the desk will eventually be seen, and the blood spilled as of late is worse than at the beginning. Stay braced, for the winds are picking up according to My command, and the stakes have never been higher for your country or your Church." He stepped over the desk and left the room. Moments later, the desk faded into nothing. The bloodstains glowed red before sinking through the floor and leaving a hole with red edges.

The Sewer Rats

March 18, 2021–
April 3, 2021

Standing in the Oval Office, I could see the blood from the previous dream (The Elder) dripping through the hole it had created. Smoke rose from the hole as the blood burned through the floors into the granite below. The blood grew thicker, seeming to be alive and moving as if there was lightning blazing within it. I found myself standing in a rounded and equipped tunnel about thirty feet wide. It seemed like it ran for miles in each direction. The tunnel had auxiliary lights and bright lighting on the walls that ran down the corridor. There were also tunnels leading in other directions (like intersections) and a channel on the ground wide enough for two vehicles to drive beside one another.

Eventually, the blood from the Oval Office dripped through the ceiling and began filling the channel where cars might drive. I could now see signs on the walls of the rounded tunnels stating distances to various locations in the city and keypads to get through every half-mile. The tunnels had walkways along the sides that could fit five to seven people across. The tunnels overflowed with rats that glowed and pulsated. They were scampering in every direction. Some were even trying to climb the smooth concrete walls.

The blood was now bubbling like it was boiling. As the level of the blood rose, smoke filled the air. The rats swam around in a frenzy, climbing on top of each other in sheer panic to get out. The lights started flashing, and an emergency siren blared. The rats were horrified by the sound and began chattering, biting, and screaming at each other. The blood kept rising until it filled the entire corridor, then it began to foam. Some rats held their faces against the ceiling, while others floated dead with the current of blood.

All at once, a flash of light burst, and blood slid away in every direction until it was only as high as the walkway. I could finally see the light and feel the air from outside, and I realized that the blood had pushed itself through every manhole and building in the area.

I now stood on Pennsylvania Avenue in front of the White House. The rats ran rampant, tracking blood on the grass, streets, and sidewalks. Every significant building had bloody tracks in and out of them: the Supreme Court, the Treasury, the Smithsonian, and the National Mall. The rats invaded everything in sight. People carrying cameras with large flashbulbs were taking photos of every set of tracks. It seemed that a reporter followed each set of tracks, took pictures, and wrote notes. With each flash of photography, the rats aged. Soon their gray hair was white, and they grew weaker until they lay on their sides and died. The rats' footprints glowed until they became thick and three-dimensional. The footprints caught fire, but the flames died quickly, leaving a smoke track.

I watched a giant man walk toward the city and grab the top of the Washington Monument like a lid. As the lid lifted, the ground around the city's primary area was uprooted with it. It reminded me of the scene from the Marvel movie *Age of Ultron*, where the city of Sokovia was lifted into the air. The giant pulled the entire monument and ground up with one hand, then placed the city into a large sifter he held with the other hand. Taking both hands, he shook the sifter, and parts of the city began to shake violently and break up. The parts falling through the sifter fell back into the hole from which they came, and quickly piled up with earth, people, and debris.

After a few minutes of shaking and sifting, the only things remaining were the federal buildings linked to the city's historical precedent. Holding the sifter in his left hand, the giant reached into the sifter with his right hand, grabbed the remaining buildings, and crushed them. He squeezed them tightly until his hand began to shake. He then opened his hand to reveal crushed debris, which he blew away. The debris transformed into smoke that faded within a few seconds. Then he placed the sifter over the hole below, but there was still an immense indentation in the ground.

The Man approached me with a scale in His hand (the kind used to weigh produce). On the scale was a bowl with the world's currencies: yen, ruble, dollar, and euro. He held the scale high above His head, then threw it to the ground where it powdered and blew away with the wind. The bowl remained in His hand, and He said,

> I determine the value of what is valued, but the soul of the nation worships paper. And paper is all it will be. The time of bracing has passed, and the season of endurance is upon the Body of Christ. Endure now, endure tomorrow, and endure until the end. Wake up, stay awake, and work while it is yet day, for the night is coming, and it will be darker than you can believe.

He threw the bowl to the ground, where it caught fire with a purple flame. The fire carried towards the sifting hole. When it got there, the entire pit caught fire, and people screamed and wailed.

The Flaming Spear

April 11, 2021–
April 19, 2021

I saw a globe sitting on a stand. Though nothing touched it, it accelerated and spun until it wobbled. Then I saw two male runners on a track that stretched for miles. The runners were separated from each other by a wall that was about twenty feet high. Each runner held a spear with a fiery torch on the end, burning brightly. One runner wore a colorful outfit like that in the Olympics, and he stretched and bounced as if preparing to run. The other wore a solid white outfit but was not moving, simply standing in place without even visible breaths.

A man came into view, standing on the wall above the runners. He wore an expensive suit jacket, running shorts, and running shoes. He carried a starter pistol and said to the motionless runner in white, "You must pace yourself and win." The runner simply nodded in acknowledgment and cracked his neck. "To your mark!" cried the starter. The runner with the multicolored outfit took a running start, threw his flaming spear into the atmosphere, and took his place in line at the runner's blocks. The runner in white moved into position but did not get down on the blocks. Instead, he leaned down, tapped the end of his spear to the ground, and spit on the flame, causing it to explode and set his hair on fire. Surprisingly, he was not hurt by this. "Ready!" cried the starter. He fired the pistol, and the runners took off. The colorful runner ran quickly and determinedly while the white runner simply jogged. Because of the wall between them, neither man could see the other.

I then saw a bright, crimson calendar with crisp, white letters that had a thick, black outline. The calendar was opened to May 2021, and two bloodstained hands unrolled June, July, August, and September. As September's page touched the ground, I saw a map of Europe that glided over Russia, China, the Middle East, the Mediterranean, and Israel. Leaders from Russia, China, Israel, and Western Europe held high-powered binoculars. They watched the United States, telling individuals to write down what they saw. They grew excited, pumping their fists in the air, patting each other on the back, and waving their national flags feverishly. I noticed the national leaders were whispering in the ears of military leadership, who would get on the phone and whisper to someone else at the other end of the line.

The hands holding the calendar were now dripping blood onto it. Fires raged across America, and cities were on lockdown. Any flags at half-mast began to fade into smoke, and many military groups were on the ground directing traffic and keeping a close watch on the streets.

Back at the track, the colorful runner sprinted hard, his hand constantly brushing the wall as he repeated, "Wake them up, wake them up, wake them up." He kept his eye on the spear he had thrown that was still soaring through the air before him. By this point, he was weary and sweating profusely. Although he was almost tripping and falling as he struggled to breathe, he recovered and kept going. The other runner's outfit had darkened from white to a dingy gray. His hand was also on the wall, leaving a fire trail that followed him. He smirked and took his time. By this point, he was fully engulfed in a fire that turned his jersey red. He suddenly grabbed his spear and threw it over the wall, and it flew after the colorful runner. Then he finally started sprinting to make up all the distance he had lost by jogging.

The colorful runner looked back and increased his speed when he saw the spear on his tail, but he turned his eye back to his spear still in the air ahead of him. It was heading toward a building filled with people on their knees praying loudly. Both runners kept moving, the red-gray runner spilling fire along the wall and the multicolored runner screaming, "Wake up!"

I next saw American generals in an underground facility. Numerous phone calls were coming in on rotary phones. As the generals answered them, they instructed others in the room to position numbers on a large map of the Atlantic and Pacific oceans. The room was frantic with energy, and the people were in a state of panic. The world leaders in Europe, Russia, and Israel talked to each other with great passion and concern on their faces. "It might be our time," they said as they watched fires burning in America.

The first spear finally hit its target building and exploded into a bright, white light that streamed down over the entire country. The impact was that of a napalm storm. The soot put out some fires completely, lessened others, and failed to impact the rest at all. As visibility improved, I saw the explosion had thrown people all over the nation, and they were extinguishing the fires. The people screamed, "Wake up, stay awake! There's not much time!"

The colorful runner finally sat down, leaned against the wall, and took a deep breath. He was just on the other side of the finish line, and the Man helped him up to his feet. The gray, fiery runner lay past the finish line and was smoking like a burnt building, not moving or breathing. The Man pointed at me and said, "Warn them, for there is not much time left, and it will never be easy again. If you are not braced now, you won't make it. If you are not rooted, you will be pulled out, and the fire will never go out. Look for Me and endure until I come."

Every international leader and American general laid their phones down in unison and said, "It's time." They all sat at their desks, put their heads in their hands, and wept.

The Testing Floor

May 17, 2021–
May 21, 2021

I sat in a 1980s-style high school classroom full of men, women, and teenagers. The room had green and black chalkboards and a clock with a powerful, audible click as the second hand moved. The clock read 11:40, but the class had clearly been in session for a while, as every student was busy writing, each in their own blue book. The Man walked the rows and took notes on a clipboard of who was testing. "There is not much time left, so stay busy and finish the work," He said. At this point, I noticed that some were dressed nicely in suits and dresses while others wore jeans and t-shirts. When the clock hit 11:45, He said, "Stay focused and let nothing draw you from the work at hand."

The test takers, strained and sweaty, regularly checked the clock and watched the Man. At 11:50, an alarm sounded until 11:51. Some of the test takers stood to stretch, but the Man paced faster and watched the students in a more determined way. When the alarm rang again at 11:55, He simply stared at

Simply Dreaming

the clock for the entire minute. When the Man turned around, tears were running down His face. He took papers from the clipboard and gave each student a sheet full of the notes He had taken. They were different for each student, yet they all cried when they saw their paper.

He spoke again, "Stay focused on the task but be encouraged while you do." His pace quickened even more, and He began touching the shoulders of each person and pouring oil on their heads from a pitcher that never emptied. The oil ran down their faces and hands until it flowed into the words they wrote in their test booklets. With that, the words became flames that sparked on the arms and chests of each person. The flames remained over their hearts and painted their faces with a fiery glow, but they continued to write without any fear.

As the clock hit 11:58 and a countdown alarm sounded, the test-takers stood with their hands in the air and praised God. The alarm sounded different than the others as it was a constant, annoying sound that filled the room with its increasing volume. The Man walked around the room quickly, picking up booklets that were smoking from the fire but weren't damaged by it. He raised His voice above the noise to say, "One minute remains. Please finish the task to the best of your ability." The praise only got louder, and the pile of booklets rose into the air and vanished through the ceiling.

When the clock hit 12:00, the floor fell through and vanished, yet somehow, the people remained standing on air. They lifted their hands and raised their eyes to Heaven as they shouted the name of Jesus. The floor that fell below the people appeared to be a map of the United States, and it billowed, flowed, and rippled as it fell into the darkness below.

Outside the building, I saw groups of women standing in circles, chanting, screaming, and cutting themselves to draw blood, which they dripped onto the map. They sought its destruction and stood stubbornly against the principles of righteousness by burning crosses and Bibles. "We need no God but self!" they chanted. As they repeated this, they danced wildly but stumbled as the earth below them began to shake. They did not run or show fear. Instead, they screamed louder and cursed God with even more vigor and frenzy.

Although I was outside with the vicious women, I knew the classroom scene was taking place simultaneously because I kept hearing the clock dinging periodically. It was as if I had gone back slightly in time. As the clock ticked toward 12:00, the ladies moved faster. When it hit noon, the map and the earth they were standing on and bleeding over fell into the ground. Everyone standing on it dropped with it, falling into a giant vortex of a bottomless hole. As I looked down at the scene, I saw the hole growing deeper, and as I looked above, I saw the people in the classroom floating on air with their hands lifted in praise.

The Man approached me in the middle of the two scenes. He held a lightning bolt in His hands—a dazzling source of light that was hard to see because it was flashing and blazing like a fire. "The violent take it by force, and the Church must be violent in her faith to withstand the winds and the fight being brought against her. But I stand with you. I am watching the clock and listening for My Father's command."

The Watchmen and the Fiery Wind

June 4, 2021

I was back in the classroom from my previous dream (The Testing Floor), where I sat at a desk furiously finishing the test in front of me. I noticed the floor was transparent underneath me, and almost a hundred men stood in a circle facing out. They were dressed casually and held Bibles as they preached fiercely. Within the dream, I reflected on a prior dream—The Attack of the Wolves. Behind each man stood a woman bracing his shoulders with her hands. While the men preached, the women called out to God in a wailing cry. Everyone was engaged in such passion and intensity that they shook.

A circular boundary held back a massive crowd that screamed at the preachers and women inside. I became aware of the same clock striking and looked to see the Man walking through the room at a frenzied pace. The preachers' words came out like fire that caught the wind and flew over the massive crowd. The fire lit the hair of some who swiftly beat it out. Those who sought the fire and were consumed by it were transformed into sharing the same message as the preachers, with the same kind of fire leaving their mouths. Most of the crowd ran from the fire; only a few accepted it and changed because of it.

The safety circle disappeared, and the mob assaulted anyone declaring the gospel. They pummeled the righteous with fists and sticks, but the preaching didn't end. In fact, it grew in passion and fervor. The crowd's eyes turned red, and they began to howl.

"One minute remains," said the Man. "Please finish the task to the best of your ability."

The praise in the room got louder, and the preachers lifted their hands, loudly declaring, "Jesus is Lord, and Christ is King!"

This caused the mob's eyes to flash red, and they swarmed the circle even more. At that moment, a mighty gust of wind hurled fire over the mob, which knocked them to the ground and blinded them. The Man walked among them and declared, "You have rejected My Word and My admonitions to your own demise. Yet, even now, if you will turn to Me, I will accept you." He then turned to the sweaty, weak, and beaten preachers and said,

> Well done. You have finished the test well. The winds of opposition are here and will get stronger but remain braced and firm in your message. Do not compromise it, for they will perish if you do. Be insistent now more than ever.

Who Are You?
Mid-June 2021

I sat at my office desk with the door closed. I hardly ever have my office door closed, which made this an unusual situation. It was a sunny day outside, so the office was brightly lit. Unexpectedly, there was a knock at the door. "Who is it?" I asked. There was no answer, so I remained sitting. The knocking continued. "Who is it?" I asked again. Again, I was met with silence. At this point, I stood up from my desk and said, "I will not answer the door until I know who is there." I still received no response, yet the knocking was ceaseless.

My office has two ways out: a front door to the main office and a side door that leads to the Secret Place prayer room. The knocking came from the front door, so I opened the side door, walked through the Secret Place, and headed toward the secondary office, where I could view my front door. I found a white, bloodless hand knocking on my door. I raised my voice and asked, "Who are you?" In the process of knocking, the hand stopped and rested itself on the door.

"Who are you?" I demanded again, but the hand faded like a wisp of smoke.

Once it was gone, I went back to my office the way I came, approached the closed front door, and prayed over it. I anointed the door and asked God to protect the gate into my office. I opened the door slowly, carefully examined the main office area, walked out, shut the door, and anointed that side of the door.

I then woke up, already pondering the dream. I shared it with Cherie Goff the very next day. At the time, I thought the dream was just for me, which is why I didn't record it and share it on social media. But now, whenever I hear a knock in the office, I think of this dream. I now realize the dream's principle is foundational for the Body of Christ as a whole. We must guard the door to our heart and spirit, only opening it when we know who and what is coming through. This also implies that some doors should only be opened if we have examined the one knocking and desiring to gain entrance.

Wall Street Bartering

June 7, 2021–
June 15, 2021

The scene began with a sunny sky and Wall Street in the background. Everything looked clean, proper, and business-like. The sidewalk was lined with sellers conducting business at long, white tables. Behind the tables, I saw live chickens, a fenced area for horses, racks of eggs, tools, and various meat and food vendors. Customers stood in line to buy, trade, and barter. One man traded five twelve-gauge shells for ten small chickens. A woman traded five hammers for fifteen boxes of screws and bolts.

A gentleman wearing an expensive suit took off his Rolex watch and asked, "Can I trade this for fifteen horses?"

The man behind the table countered, "Your watch is worth thirty horses." No vehicles were on the road, but plenty of people rode their bikes and skateboards. Everyone treated each other with kindness and respect.

A frustrated woman approached the table and said, "I desperately need eggs, but I have nothing to trade for them."

Simply Dreaming

The worker behind the table grabbed ten eggs and handed them over. The woman burst into tears and hugged the kind gift-giver.

I had this same dream, down to the very last detail, for several nights in a row. Then, on June 14, I had this same dream, but with much more information involved.

In the new rendition, the sky was the same, the sun was out, and everything was familiar until I viewed the tables. Now, I saw them from behind and was looking at those who approached to barter. The tables were bowing under the weight of the items sitting upon them. The eggs on the racks were unwashed; some were cracked and dripped onto other egg cartons. The tools were slightly rusty but organized according to their intention. I noted there were no power tools. Each section of tools had between five and fifteen of each item: hammers, boxes of screws and nails, screwdrivers, hand drills, planers, shovels, rakes, and garden tools. Hoses and animal troughs sat stacked in groups of five.

No one carried a cell phone, talked on one, or even looked at one. The man trading the shells walked up, and I noticed he was barefoot, holding up his pants with one hand and holding the shells in the other. When he received the chickens, he took his shirt off and folded it into a makeshift bag to hold them. The woman trading the hammers wore pajama bottoms, a dress shirt, and a sweater. She was missing an earring, and her fake nails were only on one hand. The man trading the watch now wore a makeshift suit jacket but no dress suit or tie, and the back of his jacket was wrinkled as if he had slept in it. He had forgotten his wallet. When he took off his Rolex, he took the metal band off and broke it into smaller pieces.

In the distance, I heard thunder and saw storm clouds coming from the west. Suddenly, lightning struck the Empire State Building, and everyone bartering covered their goods, running as fast as they could into the buildings on Wall Street. The Man unfurled an umbrella and stood under it to shield

Himself from the downpour. He said, "You are not as prepared as you need to be, so hearken to My Word and brace. Don't barter with My Word, as you will come up short."

Towers, Chains, and Trains

July 12, 2021–
July 26, 2021

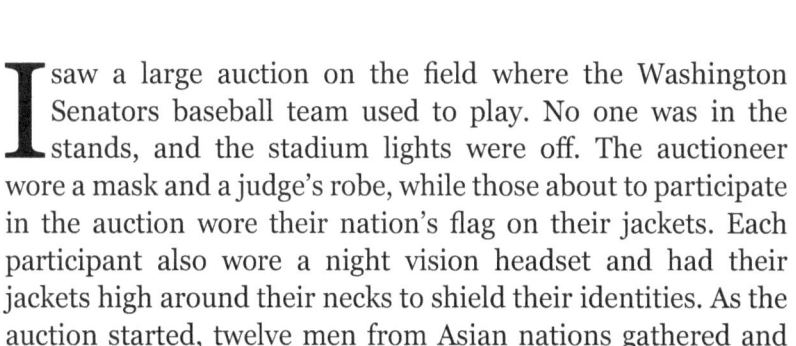

I saw a large auction on the field where the Washington Senators baseball team used to play. No one was in the stands, and the stadium lights were off. The auctioneer wore a mask and a judge's robe, while those about to participate in the auction wore their nation's flag on their jackets. Each participant also wore a night vision headset and had their jackets high around their necks to shield their identities. As the auction started, twelve men from Asian nations gathered and talked amongst themselves, then held up a card with a strange symbol, which got the auctioneer's attention.

"The auction is over," declared the auctioneer. The men from the Asian nations handed him a large briefcase. He accepted it, shook their hands, snapped his fingers, and yelled, "Now!"

At that point, I saw a hurricane-like storm surging near Indonesia. It grew in great strength as it spread fully across the Pacific Ocean. The storm turned green as it hit the west coast of the United States, then became a giant blanket of rain that covered every state as it churned its way east across the nation. The rain created torrential flooding that washed away the interstate system and melted the asphalt. When the storm reached Washington, D.C., it transformed into a tornado that drilled itself into the ground. Suddenly, the storm ceased, and the sun came out. Hundreds, perhaps thousands of snakes, slithered into the hole created by the tornado, and the Earth filled the ground on its own.

The storm's effects were devastating. I could see that America had dried up; the interstate system was now replaced with dirt roads. Somehow, the surface of the east coast seemed to be curling up towards the west coast like the metal lid of a sardine can. Underneath the dirt roads was a train or monorail system run by tracks on the ground above. The engine in front was massive. It pulled a long single-unit vehicle with a heavy chain attached. The setup reminded me of semi-trucks that connect their trailers with colorful, coiled wires. The chain at the end was attached to the roots of the east coast. As the engines chugged toward the west, the coast curled up even more and slid away with it.

I realized there were hundreds of these trains with chains pulling the nation towards the west. The activity on the surface went on as usual, simply rolling up with the curl as it impacted the people. Prison guard towers were erected and planted like seed corn over places where the land was gone. The towers had bags of white and yellow fleas inside, which they emptied gradually, causing insects to spread throughout the region. Red, muddy soil stretched across the face of the country. Towers with bright flashing yellow and blue lights stood where capital cities had once been. The Capitol Building and White House stood in what was formerly Washington, D.C., surrounded by a fifty-foot razor-wire fence.

The trains continued to pull until the surface level popped off and flew toward the sun. Just like Icarus, the skin flew higher and higher until the sun burned the coasts, which faded away. Now, trains and chains moving along the Pacific floor dragged the United States away like a wagon toward the far-east nations.

The Man appeared in the middle of the empty baseball stadium and spoke softly to me:

> Don't worry about the Red Dragon, as the Red Dragon has worse enemies than it knows. The spirit of the antichrist walks the Earth and whispers in the ears of kings at the moment. He is tempting their pride, taunting their power. And they are laying the tracks for the train of deception to pull the world into his grip. Look up, for your redemption draws near, but warn the shallow fervently that deep roots are needed now more than ever. Brace, endure, prepare, and use the time you have to reach the rootless ones.

Get Out While You Can and Take Who You Can

August 14, 2021–
August 18, 2021

I stood in front of a hospital, watching severe storms brew as tons of people rushed in with bags, luggage, and household items. An ambulance backed up to the front door, and people jumped out carrying bagged groceries. One man had nothing but an old brown grocery bag that said, "Day-old Bread." The lightning and impending rain quickened everyone's pace. The man with the bread yelled at me, "Get inside where it is safe! I have bread for everybody."

    I walked inside the building alongside the frantic people, bumping into them constantly. They ran up to different doors, dropping keys and other items as they tried to get through. Someone had put a sign on the elevator that read, "Not Working Today—Please Use Stairs." So, the people rushed up the stairs, dropping things and picking them back up as if their lives depended on them. I saw the sheer panic on every face I encountered. A few doors opened, and people asked what was going on, but those running did not respond. I ascended the only staircase, which was poorly lit and eerie.

I was then transported to the open door of a hospital room. The room had a large window in the back, through which I could see storm clouds looming outside. Thunder shook the building, and lightning struck like fire. A woman sat on the bed with her face in her hands. I recognized her as the emaciated woman from a previous dream (The Tree Grove) who was instructed to heal and get stronger before she got up. The woman sobbed and prayed about the state of the Church and the lost world. She stood up and looked out the window. Fearful of the storm, she sat down and began to shake. The booming thunder now shook the floor.

"Lord, I need to get out of here," the woman cried.

The Man appeared beside the window and replied, "I need you to work."

She kept her head down and said, "But things are crumbling around me."

He bent down and held her face in His hands. "I will go through the fire with you, but you must work now." Again, He said, "I will go through the fire with you, but you must work now." He put His hands on her head and spilled oil over her.

"Lord, how can I do this?" she asked.

"I have anointed you, and I will lead and guard you," He replied. As I stood outside as an invisible observer, I noticed smoke coming into the doorway. The Man spoke again, "Get out while you can and take who you can with you." And again He repeated, "Get out while you can and take who you can with you." He helped her get up, then disappeared right in front of her.

The woman walked to the door and covered her mouth with her sleeve, seeing a fire engulfing the hallway. A sign indicated we were on the building's fifth floor. The woman made her way carefully down the hallway and beat on doors, screaming at those inside to come out. Most doors remained closed, and the people inside yelled at her to leave them alone.

Finally, one door opened, but the man inside screamed, "Leave us alone! You should stay put for your own good. Trust in man and stay." He slammed the door shut on her.

Without giving up, the woman descended to the fourth floor and beat on more doors, begging people to follow her. By this time, parts of the ceiling were in flames and caving. A piece hit her and caught her hair on fire, but she hurriedly patted it out. Relentlessly, she continued to pound on doors. A few people hesitantly came out, covering their heads and coughing from the smoke.

"Beat on the doors and snatch them out, if need be," the woman told those joining her. So, they knocked, but few responded. The group was only six people when they descended to the third floor. Eventually, a group of forty-five to fifty made it to the bottom floor. The group was ragged and covered in soot, with their clothes torn from debris. They sweated profusely and moved even quicker than before, frantically beating on doors and begging people to leave the unsafe building.

People were still racing into the hall, heading for the main exit, when lightning struck the building, shaking it massively. Ceiling tiles fell on some of the group, and their clothes caught fire. Steel beams fell on others, and they had to be dragged out from under the debris and carried toward the door. Despite their setback, the group continued to beat on doors and cried for those still in their rooms to escape with them. The building shook again, and the woman yelled, "Get out while you can!" Everyone ran to the glass doors and poured out of the building until they hit level ground. The group was wounded, dirty, and exhausted, and above them, the ominous clouds appeared to have demonic sneers in them. The group turned to look back at the building as it continued to shake from the lightning strike.

I could see people inside the windows quietly reading and watching TV, utterly oblivious to the smoke that was blanketing their rooms. Others beat on the windows and screamed for the group to come back and help them. The group wept but did not move. Seven more people raced out of the hospital and hugged those who had knocked on their doors. The group embraced, then were startled as a deafening thunderclap sounded. The hospital collapsed, much like the Twin Towers, with dust and debris flying everywhere in a dusty cloud. When the dust finally settled, the ground was leveled, and the group had disappeared.

The Man stood where the group had been. "The setting sun is soon, and the work for the Bride on this side will end," He told me. "Go into the highways and the byways quickly. Knock on every door, for I am coming soon."

The Specialist
Early September 2021

As I sat in a doctor's office at the local clinic in Burkesville, the doctor explained that I had pneumonia and outlined the timeline for healing. "A specialist will be in to see you in a few moments," the doctor said. "While you're waiting, watch the medical information on the TV."

The room darkened, and the screen revealed running ticker tape that said things like, "Avoid the unvaccinated. These people are dangerous. Please inform authorities of all sightings."

The screen showed a group of eight people, including adults and children, as well as dogs, running along a ditch near a field of unharvested corn as the sun was setting. The group carried backpacks and several large earth-brown tarps. They had two scouts ahead of them and two hanging behind who were closely watching the road. When lights appeared on the street in either direction, the group sprinted about thirty feet into the field, covered themselves with the tarp, and lay still. They made no movement or noise until the vehicle passed. Once the threat had passed, the group emerged and ran straight ahead until they reached a T in the road. The scouts crossed to the other side of the road, where a railroad track lay on a slight embankment. They flashed lights to indicate it was safe to cross, and the group hustled over. By this point, it was completely dark outside.

A small home with an attached garage sat about fifty feet from the tracks. A light shone through the window of the garage. The scouts responded by moving a few people toward it at a time, crawling as flat to the ground as possible. After the entire group made it through the window and it closed, helicopters showed up with searchlights spotlighting the road and the ground the group had just been on.

The scene on the TV blazed with an EMS alert. The reporter stated, "Martial law has been declared. Anyone caught outside after the curfew of 7:00 p.m. will be arrested and taken to their local COVID Authority Bureau (CAB) for processing and receive a fine of up to $10,000. If you see something, say something. Safeguard your community from the dangerous assailants by doing your country proud and turning them in."

The next screen showed people being hog-tied, thrown into the backs of cattle trucks, and driven away. The people inside screamed at their handlers, but the handlers were well-armed and had cattle prods to push the captives back.

The screen then showed a medical laboratory where professionals in white lab coats and face shields stood watching a glass tube the size of a hot tub as it filled with blood. Lasers shot into the blood. The blood churned as if boiling, and although it changed colors slightly, it remained vivid and dark. Four people lay strapped on beds in the room, restrained at their necks, chests, hips, feet, and hands. They showed no fear even though they were clearly sick or dying. One of the lab assistants dipped a pitcher into the vat of blood, poured it into four smaller cups, and wiped them clean from the bottom. One caretaker from each of the four people came forward, grabbed a cup, and poured a few drops on the forehead of their assigned patient. They waited as each person moved and moaned, then asked how they felt.

One older lady said, "I feel pain leaving my hip!" and laughed. Then she began convulsing and screaming as her heart monitor beeped furiously. Moments later, she was dead. The caretaker made notes on a chart, not seeming one bit alarmed at the result.

The following two men were both quite young, and they shook nervously as the caretakers asked about their condition. One just said, "I feel heat in my chest and even younger in my spirit!" when his mind snapped, and a stroke overtook him. Once he stopped moving, the caretaker took notes and covered his face with a sheet.

The third young man made involuntary muscle movements that shook his bed. When his muscles settled, he would rest, going in and out of consciousness. "We should take him to the second observation room since we seem to have success there," noted the caretaker.

The last young woman begged, "Please don't do anything more to me!" but the caretaker gave her a shot and simply watched her stroke out and die. The caretaker made a note just before the screen went blank.

The door to my room opened, and the Man walked in. "I take it that You're the Specialist?" I asked.

"You are right," He replied. "And I will explain what you have seen if you would like to understand." When I gave confirmation, He continued:

> You are seeing the present future and the coming conservative purge. The antichrist spirit is here. They have begun to make a purchase to deceive the world with healing blood that mocks the blood of Christ. This blood is not My blood and will never heal, forgive, nor restore, but they have to appear as if it has power, even if it's empty. Yet, many will

claim and empty their will to declare its worthless virtue. You cannot be unbraced anymore. Every believer is about to have their bracing revealed and the fountain uncovered. As the Specialist, I warn you to take the salve for your eyes, to stop coating your life with wine, and stay fully sober as the day has arrived for the testing of your life.

The Man touched my forehead, leaving an ashen mark with His fingerprint on it. He reached into His left jacket pocket with His right hand, took out a small white cloth, and wiped the mark off. "I am marking those who are Mine, and I will walk beside them in the fire, even though some of you here in this country will meet Me soon on the other side." He grabbed my hand until I felt goodness and virtue entering my body. Then He said, "Be faithful unto death, and I will give you the crown of life." The room went black, and I woke, shaking and crying for about ten minutes as I gathered myself.

The Desert Road

October 20, 2021–
October 26, 2021

I walked down a wet road in the middle of a desert landscape surrounded by cacti, mesas, and plateaus. The night was clear, and the full moon lit my path. On each side of the road stood two billboards, each with digital screens showing active videos. The billboards on either side were about twenty-five feet apart and aligned with the two on the other side of the road. The billboards had slanted roofs to protect them from the elements, particularly the rain that had begun to drizzle. For some reason, the rain pooled on the top of the slanted roofs instead of falling to the ground.

The road was quite slippery, despite no rain falling on it, and the sand near the road showed no indication of moisture. I could hear wolves howling just beyond the horizon in all directions. I kept my walking speed slow to watch the video montages and avoid slipping. Upon reaching each billboard, I would stop and turn to the right and left to watch the videos facing the road.

The first video to my left displayed a grocery store with armed soldiers standing guard out front. Long lines of people wearing coats, hats, and gloves waited to go inside. It was so cold that I could see their breath. The soldiers only allowed groups of five people in the store at a time. After five people went in, the next group of five could only enter once five people left the store through the other doors. As people left, the soldiers looked through each bag and, in a bright orange notebook, recorded what the people had purchased.

The billboard to my immediate right showed a green van marked "CORONER" with a Minnesota/Wisconsin Response Team sticker on the front windshield. The van trundled through two to three inches of snow until it pulled up to a house with a large red X and the number two painted on the door. The house's windows were completely iced over. Four people stepped out of the van with gloves taped to their heavy coats. They wheeled two bodies out of the house. Both were in the fetal position and blue like they had been frozen in ice.

The next video to my left showed a reporter sharing,

> The east and west coasts are under the management of FEMA due to inclement weather patterns that have destroyed some major interstates and roads. People are advised to stay home until further notice. Gas stations have been shut down by executive order, and martial law has been declared in most major cities over 25,000.

The scene behind the reporter was devastated by tornadoes. Houses and vehicles looked as if they had been shattered and tossed around like toys. The rain and sleet mixture prevented fires from burning. The streets were empty of rioters and looters.

The final billboard on my right displayed a small church, its sanctuary cold and dark. Ten people huddled in the seats, shivering and praying. The Man walked in and raised His voice to ask, "Where is the fire?" At this statement, the people covered their faces in shame and looked away. "Look at Me and stand," He said, and they did so. He held His right hand up and declared,

Where are the Pentecostals full of fire and Spirit and faith, and why are you sitting coldly and idly by while the world freezes without your fire? Give them fire and give them food. And stop having the appearance of Pentecostals while you deny the power you should walk in.

The man opened His right hand to unveil a flame. He blew on it, and the embers swirled in the air, falling upon every person's head. The fire seemed to light a reserve of oil within them. In five of the people, the fire spread to their hearts, roaring out of their chests with a mighty noise. Those five left with smoke trailing like a pillar behind them. The other five's heads were on fire, but nothing had reached their hearts. "You might as well stay here, as you have nothing burning in your hearts and, therefore, nothing to share," the Man told them.

Suddenly, I was back on the road. The sky was much darker, and the howling of the wolves seemed much closer than before. Directly in front of me was another billboard. This one was engulfed in flames that lit up the sides of the road, allowing me to see red-eyed wolves standing in the shadows where the fire hadn't reached. The flames held them at bay, but they were aggressive, growling at me. Although I was alone, I was observant and not afraid. The Man walked through the flames and stood in front of me. "What will people see in you and the Church in the days ahead if you have no fire?" He asked. "Where are the Pentecostals full of fire and Spirit and faith? I need you to be full."

The Three Dragons

December 3, 2021–
December 10, 2021

The scene opened with a clear sky and snow-covered mountains in the vast background. I could faintly see a large, red object with wings flying in the sky near the mountains. As the object moved closer, I realized it was a dragon. The dragon flew low over the land, curling its neck toward the fearful crowds below and threatening to blow fire on them. Yet, each time the dragon got ready to send forth flames, it would pause, watching as the people dropped to their knees, begging to be spared from his wrath.

Although he was ancient, the dragon moved with elegance, speed, and arrogance. It seemed the people highly respected the dragon as if some power was held over them. Separate from the fearful crowds were those who served the dragon. Each wore a vest with a crest of a red dragon. These servants pushed and beat the crowds into compliance, occasionally lifting their eyes to the dragon to confirm he saw them lead under his authority.

I looked back toward the mountains and saw a large, blue object circling slightly lower than the red dragon initially flew. As it moved closer, I realized it was a blue dragon, flying under the influence of something that caused him to swerve and almost hit the ground twice. The blue dragon looked to his followers below, who wore a sickle on their vests and bellowed, "Tell the people that they will get nothing and like it." His followers began pushing others into factories and warehouses with poles and rifles. The blue dragon landed on the ground and then sat, dozing on and off. He randomly woke now and then, demanding the people listen, or he would burn them with his breath.

Suddenly, I heard thunder and explosions and looked to the sky to see a large white object racing toward me. As it closed in, I saw a young, energetic white dragon flying with great skill and speed. He swooped all around, leaving something in the hands of every person he approached. The people had no fear and ran toward the dragon each time he appeared. Others waved their arms in an attempt to get the dragon's attention. When he saw them, he would swoop down and drop things for the people, who would clap, dance, and cry because of it. The white dragon did this consistently until he slowly and methodically sat down to sleep atop the snow-covered mountains.

The red dragon then flew high over the sleeping white dragon, but when the red dragon swooped closer, the white dragon would rise and fly after the red dragon until he fled. After each encounter, the white dragon would rest again on the mountaintop. Eventually, the blue dragon attempted the same approach, but the white dragon opened one eye and immediately chased the blue dragon away. The white dragon then began dropping items off once more to those who wanted them. As he did, though, he slowed down, his white scales turning yellow and wrinkles forming on his face. I noticed some of his talons were now broken and dull, and scars lined his body. At that point, he looked exhausted and began ignoring the calls of those requesting his help. He climbed slowly up the mountain, aging quickly, finally falling asleep when he reached the top.

The red dragon wasted no time and proceeded to fly above the white dragon once more, this time getting close enough to provoke the sleeping giant. The white dragon, however, did not move nor even acknowledge the red dragon's proximity. Suddenly, the red dragon roared to summon the blue dragon. Together, they approached the sleeping dragon and tied him up with rope around their talons.

The white dragon did not wake up.

The crowds below begged the white dragon to help them but received no answer. The white dragon lay still, eyes closed, unaware of anything happening. As the red and blue dragons secured the white dragon, he grew until he was ten times bigger than moments before. Yet, the sleeping giant was muzzled, tied to the ground, with clipped wings to prevent him from ever flying again. Finally, he awoke. His eyes bulged red, and he shook so hard it sounded like sheet metal being twisted in a storm.

"Finished and done, you are, you are," the blue dragon whispered in his ear. The white dragon fought as hard as he could against the restraints but finally gave up. He shed several tears and then closed his bulging eyes. Under the muzzle, he took a deep breath, then smoke billowed from his nostrils.

The people he had helped spit on him and walked away in disgust. The red and blue dragons laughed at the corpse. As they started to fly away, the red dragon put a leash on the blue dragon. The blue dragon snarled in anger. "Right back to where we started," said the red dragon. They took flight, the red dragon leading the way with the blue dragon following behind.

A blizzard awakened in the mountains. The Man approached me with a walking stick in each hand. He wore a soldier's outfit with a military backpack on His shoulders. He stopped in front of me and pointed to the sky, sweeping His hand over the expanse to suggest the scope of the horizon. "Get ready for a fight with those coming from above, and know that the fire in you will be necessary. Astute discernment you must use, and fully armored you must be."

He rolled up His sleeves, grabbed the backpack with His hands, then walked back toward the mountain. He looked into the sky intently, and I noticed that He had left the walking sticks behind.

The Eastern Front
December 29, 2021

I looked out over a predawn morning and saw some light in the distance. I heard someone say, "The all quiet on the eastern front is about to become chaos."

The Jets

January 7, 2022–
January 19, 2022

I sat at my office desk, watching a podcast on my computer. On my right was a window with a calendar hanging next to it. The calendar was simple; it had no pictures, and the word "January" was bolded and highlighted. As I looked out the window at the clear, sunny skies, the calendar flipped to February. When the calendar flipped to March, the skies turned dark gray, and I heard a distinct sound, like F-16s flying by the window. I couldn't see anything, though, because of the overcast sky. On the calendar, the months of April, May, June, July, and August passed with the sun shining and nothing of concern outside. When the calendar slowly turned to September, the paper became like a leaf that changed colors in the fall. When the month finally stopped moving, the sky outside was dark. I could hear the wind and random noises, and then I heard the jets again.

    A group of three F-16s flew by the window heading north. When they were directly in my line of vision out the window, they paused wingtip to wingtip, displaying flashing red and yellow lights on their tops and bottoms. After the pause, they rocketed ahead at a magnificent speed and were soon out of sight and hearing. They moved as if on a mission, which reminded me of 9/11.

Just as suddenly, three different jets flew south, pausing in the window long enough for me to note the same formation and lights until flying south as fast as the previous jets.

At this point, I got up to stand in front of the window and simply looked outside. I immediately heard jets again but couldn't see them because of the dark sky. They suddenly appeared right in front of the window, having flown from the east and heading west. They paused long enough that I could see they were side by side with a brilliant flame pouring from their rears. They picked up speed quickly and suddenly flew straight up. Almost immediately, I heard a sonic boom, so I pressed my face against the glass to see as high and far as I could, but all the jets had disappeared. Three had gone north, three had gone south, and three had started west but then flew straight up at an astonishing speed.

I peered up at the sky, perplexed, when the Man appeared in the window in front of me. He looked at me, pointed up, and said, "Up is coming, and it is beginning. All that you have braced for is now. Stay braced and ready, eyes on the prize, and be steady in your steps."

The New Cold War

January 19, 2022

After being unable to sleep, I got out of bed around 2:15 a.m. to pray. While pacing and praying, I saw the following vision: I stood on the boundary of Ukraine and Russia. I saw large, boiling pots with soldiers on both sides tossing in blocks, bricks, tree limbs, and black bags. The different sides were not interacting, just simply filling the pot. As it filled, the pot grew until it was about fifty feet high. Two walls began to grow from the boiling pot at the same height. One wall moved north and blocked Ukraine, Belarus, Latvia, and Estonia. The other moved south, closing off Russia, Georgia, and the southern part of Ukraine. Eventually, this southern wall stopped moving southward and grew taller, seeming a hundred feet high. It separated the nations from Russia, with Georgia being the exception.

The southern wall turned blue with cold and started buzzing with an electrical or digital signal. Ice then appeared on the wall, and the signal going through the wall froze in place. Between Estonia and Georgia, however, a pulse in the wall moved like the signal on a heart monitor. When nightfall came, the pulse became visible on the western side. Lights revealed guard turrets about fifty feet above the wall, one guard watching each side. I heard the words, "A new Cold War is upon us, but cyber will be the new cipher."

The Rockwell Painting
February 12, 2022

I stood in a small, rural church foyer where I studied Norman Rockwell's "Freedom from Want" painting. It hung in a simple gold frame surrounded by artificial ivy. As I stared at the picture, I was drawn into the scene and found myself sitting at the table as the grandmother brought in the turkey. The grandfather looked out the window behind him and suddenly shut the blinds, giving his wife a strange look. Gunfire and explosions abruptly sounded outside the window.

Several kids jumped up from the table to look outside, but the grandmother screamed at them. "Sit back down! Nothing is going on outside!" She drew herself back to a peaceful form. Those at the table knew something was going on, so they took out their cell phones to pull up the news.

"Put your phones away! Stay focused on our gathering!" the grandfather yelled. He kept looking back at the window each time there was a significant noise, while the grandmother just smiled at the others and kept carving the turkey. The people passed their plates to the grandmother, who filled them and gave them back.

"Everybody hold hands. I'm going to pray," announced the grandfather. A family of a man, woman, and male teenager were too busy watching the window with concern. "Focus, please, and ignore what's happening outside because nothing is," said the grandfather. He bowed his head and began to pray. As he prayed, his lips moved, but there was no sound. The house shook. Each time it happened, he'd turn his head slightly toward the window but kept his eyes shut.

The grandmother kept telling the concerned family, "Keep your eyes shut and be quiet." The noise outside got closer, and the house shook a few more times. Each time, the grandfather noticeably flinched.

"Amen!" the grandfather said. He smiled at everyone. "Let's eat and pretend it's all good." The people at the table began eating, but after a few bites, their faces betrayed that the food was awful. The grandfather loudly spoke up, clearly exaggerating when he said, "This food is so good!"

The family of three looked at each other in disgust. "No, this is really bad," one of them answered.

"Don't you talk to your pastor that way!" barked the grandmother. She threw her napkin on the table, stood up, covered all three plates in gravy, and sat back down. "That will make it easier to get it down, so stop complaining." The others chewed on their food quietly but made it obvious the food was terrible.

It was then I noticed everyone was pale, weak, and malnourished. There was a whistling sound, and the concerned family looked at the window and cried, "Everybody get down now!" The grandfather covered his face with his hands and laid his head on the table. Suddenly, the house exploded with smoke, fire, and destruction. As it cleared, I could see the table was still there, but the damage to the people in the house had been catastrophic. Everyone was dead and dismembered. The plates of food remained on the table. Despite the wreckage, the family of three crawled out from under the table and sat back down.

At the opposite end of the table from the dead grandfather sat the Man. He pointed at the family and said,

> You were wise to listen to the Word, for that is what spared you from the destruction that is here and now. Warn the Church to listen and to inspect every bite of their food. And warn those in the pulpit to stop feeding their people a lie, for I am watching, and I will destroy the poisoned well. And I will remove My light from their pulpit and the life from their eyes. Go and find fresh water and truth that will feed your souls.

The three got up, wiped the debris from themselves, and thanked Him for sparing them. "You saved yourself by recognizing the truth was not being spoken," He told them. Then He looked at me and said, "Warn the Church and keep warning the Church to seek the truth until I come."

Stopping the Machine

March 9, 2022–
March 12, 2022

I saw a huge commercial building that had a heavy-duty machine spinning in circles inside. Although menacingly large, the machine looked like a bicycle tire; its solidly-built spokes rotated with great speed. The machine was hooked to a chimney that blew thick, black smoke into the sky. It churned over the United States as if the smoke were alive. The machine's high rate of speed caused sparks of electricity and small flames to burst from it periodically. It hummed so powerfully that it sounded like a jet engine whining as it raced toward the end of the runway to take off.

    Without warning, a person brandishing an axe ran toward the machine and tried to strike a spinning circle located on the bottom-center of it. Upon contact, the man was instantly thrown about twenty feet away, and the axe in his hand was thrown even further, out of his reach. Next, a woman from the other side charged toward the machine with the same kind of axe and struck the spinning circle. She was met with the same result. Both the man and the woman lay groaning and writhing on the ground like they had been in a car wreck. The Man approached the machine, and while the spinning continued, the hum ceased. "You have to work together, as I have told you before," He said. "And you need more people to attack what is producing the darkness."

The scene changed to me looking down on the United States and watching the smoke churn quicker, like a tornado with pounding winds. I saw small fires begin in the Midwest. The stronger fires spread across the land, while the weaker ones quickly blew out. As the fires blazed, they somehow burned holes through the thick, dark smoke that still hung in the sky. Once the holes were wide enough, some fires lifted to burn above the smoke while a portion remained on the ground. The strong fires tried to contain the smoke, their blue flames appearing like hands above and below, pushing against the smoke to hold it in place. This fire and smoke battle occurred nationwide, especially in the Midwest and large coastal areas.

I appeared back in the warehouse, which was then filled with a crowd of people holding axes. As they stared at the bicycle-wheel contraption, they collectively crept toward it and stopped about five feet away on all sides. After raising their axes in unity, they cried out, "Now!" Simultaneously, the Man appeared behind the group mouthing the word along with them. The group charged the machine, and they all struck the foundation with their axes. With a loud screech, the machine stopped spinning, but the power mechanism tried to keep it alive. The people held their axes in place and strained against the machine's power but held their ground.

A sickening sound began to pulse through the building, but the people remained in position. Despite being bloodied, sweaty, and strained, they encouraged each other to stand firm and quoted Psalm 144:1 together: "Blessed be the Lord my Rock, who trains my hands for war, and my fingers for battle." By that point, the machine was whining louder and shaking harder, but the people didn't move. Finally, a large piece from the top of the circle shattered, and the machine ceased all movement and vibration. As it started smoking, the factory shut down, and all the exterior doors opened. The people grabbed their axes and followed the Man outside.

Once there, He pointed to the distance and said,

You won't stop all the evil, but together you can take down more of it. Focused prayer and unity are more important now in America than ever before. It is up to you, so find the motivation and strike the root together. Remember that evil will fight back, but I am with you and in you and greater in you than you know.

Pointing at the city on the horizon, He said, "Strike together and aim for the root."

The Distraction

April 14, 2022–
April 30, 2022

I watched a large passenger airplane with an American flag on its tail fly briskly at around 35,000 feet. The plane began to shift to the typical angle of descent. Below the plane, a blanket of clouds swirled as if the wind was blowing rapidly. The passengers on the airplane appeared unfazed by the descent, and they busied themselves reading magazines, listening to headphones, and sleeping. No one bothered to look out the windows or showed any alarm at the clouds. The plane unexpectedly accelerated to a complete nosedive. The people on board made no changes to their activity despite the plane hurtling to an explosive demise.

At this point, I watched naval ships surround Taiwan and aim heavy-caliber weapons at her. The naval ships had started far out in the water, and as they moved toward the shoreline, they gathered like a tightened knot. In mainland China, military leaders sat at a table pushing pieces on a map that indicated distinct movements. A few of them were near a red button. The leaders communicated angrily via radio and pounded their fists on the table. The main Chinese leader looked out of place as he stared at the phone in his hand and rocked nervously in an old-fashioned American rocking chair.

At a table near St. Basil's Cathedral and the Kremlin in Moscow, Putin and his military leaders sat having a picnic lunch. Their large picnic baskets and abundance of empty wine (not vodka) bottles covered the table and littered the ground around them. Putin held his side as if he was sick with severe abdominal pain. Because of this, he wasn't drinking with his men. He stared at a cell phone in his hand while sitting in the same kind of rocking chair as the Chinese leader. Unlike the Chinese leader, Putin was extremely calm, relaxed, and untouched by the boisterous generals around him.

The scene changed to Europe. Leaders there sat around a table and discussed the surrounding of Taiwan and what they could do to help. Their final decision was to let US and British leaders handle the crisis, as they all had faith those nations would figure it out. The leaders stood and shook hands while wiping sweat from their brows. Then, I saw a split screen of both the Chinese leader and Putin. They hit send on their phones simultaneously, shut their eyes, and fell asleep.

The navy ships turned from the coastline of Taiwan and began speedily untying the dragnet they had been tying moments before. Over Ukraine, a storm of missiles rained down on a larger scale than anything I have previously seen in news headlines. In western Russia, giant uncovered silos billowed smoke, but no launch occurred. I did, however, see a large rocket launch from one of the Chinese navy ships around Taiwan. It headed straight up, then took off at what could only be hypersonic speed east across the Pacific Ocean. The sky had lines showing it was heading right over the United States, but the trajectory stopped in the middle of the country.

Finally, the plane from the beginning of the dream dipped below the lowest clouds, and I could see the land patterns on the ground below. An explosion rang out above the clouds, and the plane lost all power below the canopy. At first, it appeared as if the pilot was pushing the plane toward the ground on purpose, but once the lights inside the plane went off, the passengers became aware that their music had stopped and the TVs were off. They looked out the windows in shock and horror while others screamed and beat on the pilot's door in sheer panic. In the middle of the chaos, it went completely dark.

As the plane continued its nosedive, I saw the Man sitting next to the window, looking out at me, unafraid of what was going on. Right before He disappeared, He said, "I told them to pray, but they did not. They need to take it seriously now."

The Millstone

May 20, 2022–
May 27, 2022

I stood in an open field while the sun blazed at high noon. In my left hand, I grasped a silver metal staff that was at least a foot taller than me. In my right hand, I held a compass that pointed west. In front of me, I observed a giant stone hanging in midair at a high altitude. The stone was square, with a large round hole near the top that had a rope tied through it. I began walking west toward the stone. The field where I stood seemed like a combine had just gone through it. The grass was green and healthy in most places, but it was turning brown and dead where it had recently been cut.

The stone suddenly began to descend, but there was no fiery entry through the atmosphere nor any sound except the whipping of the rope trailing behind it that seemed to be hundreds of miles long. The rope sounded like unsecured cargo inside a vehicle that was speeding down the highway. The stone fell very quickly, and I began to feel the wind coming from it as it got closer. I then realized I was as far west as possible;

there was a sign next to me that said, "Pacific Ocean." At that point, the stone was the size of Texas and shadowed the entire western half of the United States. As it continued to fall, I heard the whipping of the rope behind it, which hung from the blank space above and appeared to be many miles wide.

The stone crashed in the middle of the ocean, but I heard no violent splash. Instead, it just eased into the water and sank. The broad daylight faded over the next few minutes, and the rope kept falling from the sky, forming a circle around the United States. As the stone sank, the rope tightened around the country's shores until the Midwest appeared to display a choking face and was having trouble breathing. I could hear an unsteady, choppy, violent heartbeat somewhere. Then I heard the millstone hit the bottom of the Pacific Ocean. As it did, the Midwest took a deep breath as the noose around the nation loosened slightly. The face smiled with relief for a few seconds.

The Man's face superimposed over the Midwest's face. He took a deep breath and said, "This is for the slaughter of and the hands that shed innocent blood." I saw the stone on the ocean floor being harshly pushed through the Earth's mantle by a hand. The rope tightened so quickly around the nation that the whole place shook violently and went suddenly still. There were severe earthquakes across the country, and smoke rolled before the face took its last breath. What got my attention was the speed at which the nation seemed to die.

I then saw a horse and its rider, the Man, dressed in gleaming white. He pointed to the destruction and said, "I keep My Word, and I will be faithful to keep My Word as it regards the blessing and the curse. There is not much time to work, and those who know, know this deeply. Get busy, stay busy, and know that I am coming very soon."

In a flash, the horse and rider were gone, and I was left standing back in the field where I started. I noticed the season had changed; the crops were ready to be harvested. The fields were ripe, but only a few in the field were working. I was overcome with despair, but then large groups of people from every direction started coming with large bags over their shoulders and old-fashioned sickles in their hands.

The shadows began to shade the field, but the sun was still up, so the workers started running at full speed toward the fields. With a flash of light, the Man stood before me and warned, "It's too late to start bracing, and the braced are about to be tested harshly, so lock in place."

Precision

June 15, 2022–
July 3, 2022

I found myself standing in a shipping yard where large containers were being lifted off ships. A sign close to me indicated I was in the port of Los Angeles. I saw eight jet-black containers placed on the ground about fifteen feet apart, each pristine and marked with Chinese letters. The letters were about five by five feet with a brown background that made them look 3D. Because it was still light outside, I could see a clock tower looming high above the shipping facility. At exactly 3:00, all eight containers' doors began to bang and shake violently before bursting open. A man in military equipment rode out of the first container on an oversized green dirt bike with large, knobby tires and leather saddlebags on either side of the seat.

    The man took off his helmet, revealing that he was Asian. He put the kickstand down, stepped off the bike, and began screaming at the trucks while pointing in different directions. His face was beet red with fury when he stopped to check his watch. He then put his helmet back on, returned to his motorcycle, and started it. Simultaneously, the clock struck 4:00, a deep bell

Simply Dreaming

rang, and the Earth shook. Out of each container came about twenty-five soldiers riding the same kind of motorcycles with AK-47s over their backs. At this point, I could see RPGs plus lots of ammunition and weapons in their saddlebags. When the first soldier hurried from the port, the rest followed, but they went in different directions once they were out of the fence line.

The scene changed, and I heard news reports and saw newspaper headlines with serious-faced reporters announcing deaths all over the country. The reports shared that water systems were being poisoned in random rural and metropolitan areas. The poisonings had affected the West more than anywhere else in the country. One headline read, "Entire Communities Poisoned Through Water Supply." Reporters told listeners to drink nothing but bottled water they knew was not connected to the local water supply. They promised there were fully armed national guard units watching water facilities. Thousands were reported as having died, hospitals were full of heavily poisoned people getting medical treatments, and FEMA centers were being set up in the affected regions. An Emergency Broadcast announcement ran along the screen, saying, "Boiling water is not an effective way to make any water safe."

I saw the clock tower standing above a municipal water supply with its hands pointed to 4:05 in the afternoon. I then saw people in airports and shopping centers all watching TVs, completely shocked by what they were seeing. The rooms were full of gasps, tears, and covered mouths as people held tightly to each other in fear of what they saw on the screens.

Next, I saw four lines of lights that seemed to be coming up from the border, which reminded me of a video of the Ho Chi Minh Trail. Although many people were coming from the border, it happened in an organized way. The people moved east hundreds of miles from California to Texas with their lights bright enough to be seen from space. They all stopped moving at once, and when they did, smaller light trails from within the

US started moving toward them. Together it was like watching moths drawn to a flame. The source light increased until it flashed, indicating that all the smaller lights were attached. For a few moments, everything went dark. Then the lights pulsed and exploded, which spread it hundreds of miles. Now the clock tower stood high above the ground and showed that it was 4:10. Small embers of flames showered down around the clock, but they didn't catch the ground on fire even though it looked like they should have.

A sudden silence permeated the atmosphere. When the clock struck 4:15, an alarm sounded across the nation. The scene changed again. I saw churches of all shapes and sizes surrounded by screaming mobs of people who chanted hostile threats from a considerable distance. I heard people inside the churches leading others in prayers, but their prayers had no power or authority, so the crowds kept surging. In at least five locations, I saw arrows fired from the church roofs into the mobs, which scattered them. As the people scrambled, I noticed an archer on each roof. Somehow, it appeared to be the Man firing the arrows in each location at precisely the same time. The alarm finally stopped as the Man walked toward me.

He had a quiver over His shoulder full of sheer, white arrows with extremely sharp points. He grabbed a long bow and stood it on the ground. He was silent for a few moments as He surveyed the area. Then He turned to me and spoke:

> There must be precision in your prayers from this point forward; absolute precision to counter the noise and the violence that will be aimed at the Body. The Church must remember that it is not by might nor by power but by My Spirit that will help you walk straight through the battle. There must be precision and power in your prayers—there *must* be. The war has arrived, and those awake are on the front lines now, and you will never be able to get away from that line. Absolute precision is required in your prayers.

After saying this, He quickly put an arrow into the bow and shot it straight into the air. The arrow never came back down, but He kept looking into the air where He shot it. He never looked back at me as He said, "Remember to be precise, as it matters more than ever right now." Then He disappeared before my eyes.

"Hail to the Chief"
August 6, 2022

I stood watching a TV broadcast of the 2023 State of the Union Address. The usual leaders were already sitting in the room, waiting for everything to start. The Sergeant at Arms introduced the President in a whisper, then coughed harshly and clutched his chest as if he was having trouble breathing. The song "Hail to the Chief" began to play over the loudspeakers, and the audience turned in anticipation for the President to enter. Although there was thunderous applause, the President didn't come through the chamber. The audience looked around in confusion, straining to see where the President was. The music continued to play but gradually increased in volume until the decibel level made everyone cover their ears.

Secret Service agents with white earpieces pulled their weapons and surveyed the crowd in alarm. As they searched every square inch of the room, they spoke into small microphones on their wrists and collars. More Secret Service agents ran in through the very door where the President was supposed to have entered moments before. They, too, looked around in alarm and moved quickly to assess and get intel on the situation. The crowd began to panic with absolute fear in their eyes. Various party leaders attempted to get onto the platform to ask what was going on, but security teams had already walled it off, so they had to sit back down.

An official black-jacketed agent stormed past the Secret Service agents and crowd and yelled, "Everyone sit down immediately!" This agent didn't have the typical white earpiece worn by Secret Service agents, but he carried himself as if everyone should have known him. "Shut that music down!" he demanded. When no one turned it off, he pulled his weapon, pointed it, and fired it at an acoustic speaker at the back of the room. The music stopped immediately. People screamed, and the agent shouted again, "Everyone sit down immediately!" A new group of men entered the room and filled the area between the seats. I sensed they weren't Secret Service, but they all wore full body armor with military gear and weapons. These were no soldiers, but they had the weapons and vests of soldiers over their two-piece suits.

"Ladies and gentlemen, we have lost the President," the black-jacketed agent proclaimed.

The crowd riled up quickly, and I heard shouts of, "What do you mean?" and "How did that happen?"

The agent lifted his hands and made a lowering motion to keep the crowd under control. Then he said, "You all knew this would happen, and now that it has, you will either support the consequences or join the missing. Please stand, raise your right hand, pledge allegiance, then kneel when you are told."

I heard the gavel rap loudly on the desk in the congressional chamber where the President would have addressed the nation. People looked around but did not move. Several had their heads down with their eyes closed, while others were full of tears, and the rest were visibly shaking.

The man at the front screamed, "I said stand!" He held the word "stand" until it rang across the room. A few men and women stood and turned toward the back door. Several people still sitting screamed in protest. As soon as they did, the men in military suits stood behind them, held syringes to their necks, and injected something. Within seconds, those people had slumped to the ground as if dead. This caused the crowd to gasp and scream in panic—even the men, who were then weak-kneed and struggling to get to their feet. The looks of terror on their faces were horrible. It seemed like they were facing a death sentence, sobbing as they stood to turn and face the door. The men in military outfits quickly disposed of those who would not stand as requested or resisted, butting them with AR-15s and injecting them. Everyone who stood did so at a slow pace, and the slowest were some of the highest elected officials and Supreme Court Justices in the front row.

A thin Asian girl walked in the back door with a flute. She began to play a haunting melody that was high-pitched and sharp to the ears. She marched with military precision as she headed toward the podium. When she was about ten feet from it, she jumped with incredible acrobatic skill and held the last note for what seemed like minutes. Then she stated, "You said you were with us; now we see." The room filled with the sound of the audience weeping.

Suddenly, all sound faded from the room, and the Man stood at the podium. He addressed the crowd, "And it all took place in less than 250 years." He looked at me where I stood just off the right corner of the podium and said, "Get ready for more than war and speak the truth at risk of the sword."

The Canary in the Coal Mine

December 1, 2022 -
December 5, 2022

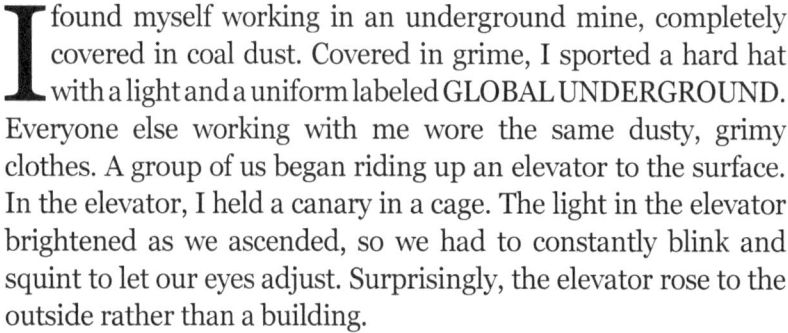

I found myself working in an underground mine, completely covered in coal dust. Covered in grime, I sported a hard hat with a light and a uniform labeled GLOBAL UNDERGROUND. Everyone else working with me wore the same dusty, grimy clothes. A group of us began riding up an elevator to the surface. In the elevator, I held a canary in a cage. The light in the elevator brightened as we ascended, so we had to constantly blink and squint to let our eyes adjust. Surprisingly, the elevator rose to the outside rather than a building.

    Before getting out, I looked around and realized that Jesus had ridden with us to the top. As we got out, a new crew stepped into the elevator to descend. Jesus approached me and pointed at the canary. "Pay attention to details more than you ever have. Go back down with the next crew and be sure to take the canary." I turned around and crowded back into the elevator with the new crew. I immediately noticed I was the only one covered in coal dust, disheveled, and weary. This new crew was clean and fully awake.

As the elevator began its descent, someone raised their voice and asked with alarm, "Where's the guy with the canary?"

I raised the cage with the canary and said, "I'm here."

"No, where is the one assigned to the next crew? You just came up." He seemed pretty concerned. "The guy assigned to this shift, where is he?"

"I was told to go back down with this crew and to be sure to take the canary," I replied.

As the elevator continued going down, the man squeezed through the crowd until he was right next to me and said, "You're not assigned to this crew, so who told you to come down?"

"Jesus told me to."

He looked at me very seriously, then burst into exaggerated laughter, saying firmly, "Well, I'm telling you to leave." He tried to grab the cage out of my hands, and things quickly escalated. The man pushed and fought me as the other men in the elevator tried to get out of the way. I was getting slapped and beaten, but I kept my grip on the cage. The bird remained on its perch and made no noise despite the altercation.

I held on and kept fighting back. The man grew more aggressive, so I finally yelled, "I'm not letting go of this cage!" Since the fight took place in such a small space, it created an awkward situation for everyone else. I knew I had to position myself in the corner, and when I did, I held the cage toward the corner, trying to shield it with my body.

Since I had exposed my back, the man pounded on it, but I still held the cage tightly to protect the bird. The man continued hitting me until I heard Jesus say in my head, "Let the bird out." In between blows, I argued with Jesus in my thoughts, telling Him this was not a good idea.

The elevator finally reached the bottom level, the doors opened, and the other men left quickly. I opened the front of the cage and dropped to the ground to avoid more blows. The bird flew out and around the head of the man hitting me. He began to yell and curse but couldn't catch the bird in his grip. Finally, the canary grabbed the man by the nostrils with its talons and stared right into his eyes, making him freeze in terror.

The bird let go of the man to fly back in and out of the cage again. It seemed that he was telling me to follow him. The workers who had come down on the elevator with me were in place, working in their areas with shovels and wheelbarrows, loading up small train cars with coal. The canary flew to each man's ears and sang an encouragement. Suddenly, the man who had attacked me showed up, yelling at people and swatting at the bird. The men continued working but were cautious of their angry coworker. They didn't try to harm him, but they started singing out loud, which enraged him so much that he threw chunks of coal at them. The crew simply worked through it.

One of the men walked up to me with a shovel in his hand. When he removed his hat, I recognized him as the Man. He wiped His face on a cloth and handed it to me, saying,

Somebody has to take the light to the dark places, and there are those who will not like the light that you bring, but they can extinguish the flame that I started in your hearts. Burn brilliantly and with passion; fight the good fight and remain grounded in the Word because the world is about to go dark. And that dark world will need the light you carry to reveal the way to Me.

He returned to work alongside the other men, and the canary landed on His shoulder. He turned to me and said, "Go and encourage the crew that is coming down the shaft and tell them I will be working beside them in the dark."

The Headlines, the Sheep, and the Goats

January 2, 2023–
January 24, 2023

I saw many newspapers' pages rapidly flipping through with the headlines visible on each page. Each publication had the words 8 Billion or the number 8,000,000,000 on their respective front pages. Soon other headlines began to appear that highlighted high crime, poverty, and world chaos. I saw headlines about school violence, of teachers locking themselves in rooms and calling 911 to be rescued from marauding gangs of violent students. I saw headlines of food shortages and starvation, of people leaving cities for the safety of rural communities, while those stuck in cities had armed and barricaded themselves in their homes. I saw highways lined up for miles with cars, many of which had run out of gas, leaving those families stranded and begging for help.

After each headline, the number 8 billion would appear again, and I would see more nations where the same chaos was occurring. People were struggling to provide for and protect themselves. The crime was utterly out of control. One particular headline read, "Washington Paralyzed in Nationwide Crime Wave." I saw a field with people from around the world standing in a tight circle and looking up at the sky. The headlines returned: "Weather Anomalies Questioned," "Death Rates Unparalleled in 2023," and "College Lost at Sea." The field returned, and the people still looked up with more expectation than before. More headlines scrolled through: "Banks Becoming Regionalized—60% of Bank Branches to Close by 2027," "Summer Is Not Coming," as well as "President Who?" and "Mattresses Useless Now—Cash Not Worth Hiding."

The atmosphere suddenly changed, and the sky became extremely bright. I saw another field packed full of white sheep and gray goats. The sheep were looking up and around, watching everything cautiously, while the goats were oblivious to their surroundings and constantly bumping into other animals. There was a faint darkening of the skies, and I saw the Man approach the gate at the front of the field. He walked up quietly with a shepherd's staff in his right hand and gazed at the animals inside the fence. The goats paid Him no attention, but the sheep began to walk toward the gate, some moving quicker than others. The Shepherd opened the gate and firmly said, "Come."

At once, the sheep began lining up and walking through the gate. The Shepherd moved the staff to His left hand and knelt to one knee. As each sheep passed by Him, He drew the sheep near and embraced it as it nuzzled close to His chest. Then the sheep went on.

At one point, a goat tried to get in line. The Shepherd walked over, grabbed it by the horns, and steered it away from the gate. He tapped the ground with the staff and pointed it at the goats, then walked back to the gate and waved the sheep forward. "Come," He said again.

I watched as hundreds of sheep were embraced and then walked next to the Shepherd. He looked at me and said, "Get ready to get in line, for I am coming soon. The Spirit and the Bride say 'Come,' and I say 'Soon.'" At this, the sky turned a brilliant white with a beautiful blue hue. The sheep began to dance and jump, and I heard angelic voices worshipping the God of the universe.

These Are Additional Headlines I Saw in My Dream:

- Sex Crime Units Overwhelmed in Southern Big Cities
- Rampant STDs Killing Elderly
- The Zombie Apocalypse—New Drugs Turning Users into Walking Dead
- Who Is Killing Unelected Movers in the Political and Medical World?
- Govts Tracking Assassination Teams Crossing Borders
- Gun Grabs Lead to Standoffs Nationwide
- Pagans R Us Lead the Polls
- Underground Spy Network Links Congress to White House
- Cancel the Cross Events Hosted in Democratic Cities
- Unholy Trinity of DC Leaders Intends to Ease Morality Definitions
- Gates, WHO, and WEF Fix Standards—Medical Tyranny on Steroids
- Launched—Poke the Bear, Face Incineration
- The West Knows What It Is Doing—They Have Swallowed The Pill and Got It Down with Poison

About the Author

Dana Coverstone has been an Assemblies of God pastor for over thirty years and has been preaching since he was sixteen. He and his wife, Jennifer, have been married for over twenty-eight years and have three adult children. He holds an MA in Expository Preaching and previously published a book called *Simple Accountability*. He enjoys reading, studying, and being around people. He has visited many countries and has a big heart for missions, especially Speed the Light. He is pictured here with his daughter, Keilah, who assisted him with the compilation and editing of this book.

Acknowledgments

The dreams brought an indescribable amount of craziness to my life, and I want to thank and recognize those who helped me navigate my way through it.

First of all, the guys I pray with every Tuesday and my weekly accountability partners. They heard about the dreams from the beginning and prayed for wisdom and discernment in how they were presented.

Stan Johnson from The Prophecy Club was the first person to speak to me with confidence and support after I shared the first dream publicly. His phone call on a Sunday night helped me to stay strong against the criticism and see that the dream was from God.

John Redenbo was the first person to interview me and help me understand the intel side of dreams, which is truly bigger than you think.

Cherie Goff reached out to me and has remained a steady help with the dreams that have continued to come. Her prayers have helped me gain understanding and find my footing in the process.

Jay Caprietta helped me see what was coming and prepared me for the podcasts and websites. I am thankful for his help along the way.

My church family dealt with a steady flow of people every Sunday morning service since the first dream was released, so they were baptized in response to the dreams. I'm grateful for their love and support as their pastor. Our office workers were overwhelmed by the phone calls and mail, but they handled it with joy and efficiency.

I have done countless interviews, spoken at churches and to individuals, and made friends from all over the world, but I appreciate those who prayed for me and encouraged me as well.

And finally, my wife and kids. Well, what can I say but that they were phenomenally patient and accepting of the changes the dreams brought into our lives. I have only kept sharing the dreams because I know they were from God and because my family and church family were standing with me.

At times it was a circus, but I would never change a thing. I will always cherish the lessons I learned and the friends I made along the way.

Prophetic Words from the Dreams

Editor's Note: In this appendix, prophetic words are any piece of dialogue from a spiritual voice, such as the White Figure, the Man, and God the Father. At times of ambiguity, the speaker is listed as an unidentified voice. The prophetic words are listed in order by dream and speaker. In cases when the same speaker gives multiple prophetic words, they are separated by order of appearance within the dream.

The Pandemic
- *The White Figure*:
    - "Brace yourself, brace yourself, brace yourself."

The November Fist Punch
- *The White Figure*:
    - "Part two, part two."
    - "Brace yourself, brace yourself, brace yourself."

The Coin Shortage
- *Unidentified Voice*:
    - "Brace yourself, brace yourself, brace yourself."

The Solemn September Assembly
- *Unidentified Voice*:
    - "Stand on September and pray for the Church to have

a strong backbone, for corruption to be exposed, and for a great harvest in the coming months."
- o "Get help, as you alone are not enough."
- *The Lord*:
  - o "Arise, My Bride, arise, My Bride, and prepare to pray. Arise, My Bride, arise, My Bride, and prepare for battle. Arise, My Bride, arise, My Bride, and prepare to see My face. For I am coming soon, and My reward is with Me."

The Demonic Sleeper Cells

- *The White Figure*:
  - o "Brace yourself, brace yourself, brace yourself."

October 2020

- *The White Figure*:
  - o "Do not stop bracing, for the storm will not pass until I stop the storm. So, brace, brace, brace yourselves, and don't look back."

The Three Assassination Attempts

- *Unidentified Voice*:
  - o "Those who refuse to get ready will be wanting in the end. So, brace yourself and tell others that I have warned them to brace themselves, for they are about to see even more shocking things."

The Final Warning

- *The White Figure*:
  - o "Ready or not, nation, here it comes. Brace yourself."

The Emergency Shelters

- *The White Figure*:
  - "Remain braced as this calm comes before a gathering storm that recovery will have a hard time finding."

The Harsh Winter

- *The White Figure*:
  - "Brace yourself. Brace, brace, brace yourself on the Word and My promises, and do not rely upon your own strength."

The Tree Grove

- *The Man*:
  - "Your strength has not returned yet. Soon."
  - "You need time to rest. Do not ask Me again."
  - "Do not try to walk too soon, or you will limp. You need to be able to stick to the instructions, or you will be ineffective later on. Stay braced and occupy until I come."

The Data Lines

- *The Man*:
  - "A house divided against itself *shall* not stand."

Hold Your Breath

- *The Man*:
  - "Stay braced, but don't breathe just yet."

Benjamin Franklin

- *God the Father*:

Simply Dreaming

- o "No, it's Mine now, as is the whole Earth."
- o "It's still being pressured for now but will be released in good time. Keep your glasses on, your eyes sharp, and stay committed to the captain."

Abraham Lincoln's Assassination

- *The Man*:
  - o "They didn't have any idea what they were doing, and now the nation needs to brace itself for what it deserves."
  - o "Rest in peace, Uncle Sam. Sorry you had to see the ship go down."
  - o "Nation, brace yourself for fire and ice, and don't forget to anchor your soul."

The Church and the State

- *The Man*:
  - o "You never wanted the Church to succeed, but the gates of Hell will not stop her. And those who have seen the root will prune the vine and cut off the poisonous part."
  - o "Be about My Father's business. Stay pure and fear not the State, for they know not what they do."
  - o "Stay braced, stay focused, and stay on task, for I am coming soon."

The Birds and the Maul

- *The Man*:
  - o "Justice for all is coming but will not be seen by the many who needed it desperately. Bracing is required to stay the course, but it will be a course of consequence."

The Plumb Line
- *The Man*:
  - "My plumb line never moves."
  - "To do My business."
  - "Follow me."
  - "I warned them."
  - "You took warning and were good to do so. Your obedience has been noted, and there will be fruit both here and in Heaven. Though shaken and broken, you will arise, My Bride, and work until I come."

They Don't Hate Me; They Hate You
- *The Man*:
  - "The harvest is full, but not enough are helping."
  - "I never said to stop bracing."
  - "Stay braced for His name's sake."

The Bunker
- *The Man*:
  - "Bracing will save many but will also speak to many. They will hunt you, and when you stand before the haters, I will prompt your words to convict their hearts. It has started, and darkness is in the winds, so brace and speak. And don't stop speaking."

The Mud
- *The Voice of God*:
  - "Work with the mud you have been given."
  - "Work with the mud you have been given."
- *The Man*:
  - "My ways are not your ways. Your spiritual legs will be strengthened through agony, and your witness

will offend the naïve and those who have no fear of Me. Bracing gives way to fire, and those braced must remain on the path. My command is to come out from among them, separate yourself, as the chaff is about to burn, and the smoke will fill the skies."
- o "I am coming soon, and My reward is with Me. Stay faithful until I come."

Air Force One

- *Unidentified Voice*:
  - o "Autopilot has been engaged, but do not expect a smooth ride even once we land."

The Elder

- *The Man*:
  - o "Don't let the suit fool you or the office either. What's under the desk will eventually be seen, and the blood spilled as of late is worse than at the beginning. Stay braced, for the winds are picking up according to My command, and the stakes have never been higher for your country or your Church."

The Sewer Rats

- *The Man*:
  - o "I determine the value of what is valued, but the soul of the nation worships paper. And paper is all it will be. The time of bracing has passed, and the season of endurance is upon the Body of Christ. Endure now, endure tomorrow, and endure until the end. Wake up, stay awake, and work while it is yet day, for the night is coming, and it will be darker than you can believe."

The Flaming Spear

- *The Man*:
  - "Warn them, for there is not much time left, and it will never be easy again. If you are not braced now, you won't make it. If you are not rooted, you will be pulled out, and the fire will never go out. Look for Me and endure until I come."

The Testing Floor

- *The Man*:
  - "There is not much time left, so stay busy and finish the work."
  - "Stay focused and let nothing draw you from the work at hand."
  - "Stay focused on the task but be encouraged while you do."
  - "One minute remains. Please finish the task to the best of your ability."
  - "The violent take it by force, and the Church must be violent in her faith to withstand the winds and the fight being brought against her. But I stand with you. I am watching the clock and listening for My Father's command."

The Watchmen and the Fiery Wind

- *The Man*:
  - "One minute remains. Please finish the task to the best of your ability."
  - "You have rejected My Word and My admonitions to your own demise. Yet, even now, if you will turn to Me, I will accept you."
  - "Well done. You have finished the test well. The winds of opposition are here and will get stronger

but remain braced and firm in your message. Do not compromise it, for they will perish if you do. Be insistent now more than ever."

Wall Street Bartering

- *The Man*:
  - "You are not as prepared as you need to be, so hearken to My Word and brace. Don't barter with My Word, as you will come up short."

Towers, Chains, and Trains

- *The Man*:
  - "Don't worry about the Red Dragon, as the Red Dragon has worse enemies than it knows. The spirit of the antichrist walks the Earth and whispers in the ears of kings at the moment. He is tempting their pride, taunting their power. And they are laying the tracks for the train of deception to pull the world into his grip. Look up, for your redemption draws near, but warn the shallow fervently that deep roots are needed now more than ever. Brace, endure, prepare, and use the time you have to reach the rootless ones."

Get Out While You Can and Take Who You Can

- *The Man*:
  - "I need you to work."
  - "I will go through the fire with you, but you must work now. I will go through the fire with you, but you must work now."
  - "I have anointed you, and I will lead and guard you."
  - "Get out while you can and take who you can with you. Get out while you can and take who you can with you."
  - "The setting sun is soon, and the work for the Bride

on this side will end. Go into the highways and the byways quickly. Knock on every door, for I am coming soon."

The Specialist

- *The Man*:
  - "You are right. And I will explain what you have seen if you would like to understand."
  - "You are seeing the present future and the coming conservative purge. The antichrist spirit is here. They have begun to make a purchase to deceive the world with healing blood that mocks the blood of Christ. This blood is not My blood and will never heal, forgive, nor restore, but they have to appear as if it has power, even if it's empty. Yet many will claim and empty their will to declare its worthless virtue. You cannot be unbraced anymore. Every believer is about to have their bracing revealed and the fountain uncovered. As the Specialist, I warn you to take the salve for your eyes, to stop coating your life with wine, and stay fully sober as the day has arrived for the testing of your life."
  - "I am marking those who are Mine, and I will walk beside them in the fire, even though some of you here in this country will meet Me soon on the other side."
  - "Be faithful unto death, and I will give you the crown of life."

The Desert Road

- *The Man*:
  - "Where is the fire?"
  - "Look at Me and stand."
  - "Where are the Pentecostals full of fire and Spirit and

faith, and why are you sitting coldly and idly by while the world freezes without your fire? Give them fire and give them food. And stop having the appearance of Pentecostals while you deny the power you should walk in."
- o "You might as well stay here, as you have nothing burning in your hearts and, therefore, nothing to share."
- o "What will people see in you and the Church in the days ahead if you have no fire? Where are the Pentecostals full of fire, and Spirit, and faith? I need you to be full."

The Three Dragons
- *The Man*:
  - o "Get ready for a fight with those coming from above, and know that the fire in you will be necessary. Astute discernment you must use, and fully armored you must be."

The Eastern Front
- *Unidentified Voice*:
  - o "The all quiet on the eastern front is about to become chaos."

The Jets
- *The Man*:
  - o "Up is coming, and it is beginning. All that you have braced for is now. Stay braced and ready, eyes on the prize, and be steady in your steps."

The New Cold War

- *Unidentified Voice*:
    - "A new Cold War is upon us, but cyber will be the new cipher."

The Rockwell Painting

- *The Man*:
    - "You were wise to listen to the Word, for that is what spared you from the destruction that is here and now. Warn the Church to listen and to inspect every bite of their food. And warn those in the pulpit to stop feeding their people a lie, for I am watching, and I will destroy the poisoned well. And I will remove My light from their pulpit and the life from their eyes. Go and find fresh water and truth that will feed your souls."
    - "You saved yourself by recognizing the truth was not being spoken."
    - "Warn the Church and keep warning the Church to seek the truth until I come."

Stopping the Machine

- *The Man*:
    - "You have to work together, as I have told you before. And you need more people to attack what is producing the darkness."
    - "You won't stop all the evil, but together you can take down more of it. Focused prayer and unity are more important now in America than ever before. It is up to you, so find the motivation and strike the root together. Remember that evil will fight back, but I am with you and in you and greater in you than you know."
    - "Strike together and aim for the root."

The Distraction

- *The Man*:
    - "I told them to pray, but they did not. They need to take it seriously now."

The Millstone

- *The Man*:
    - "This is for the slaughter of and the hands that shed innocent blood."
    - "I keep My Word, and I will be faithful to keep My Word as it regards the blessing and the curse. There is not much time to work, and those who know, know this deeply. Get busy, stay busy, and know that I am coming very soon."
    - "It's too late to start bracing, and the braced are about to be tested harshly, so lock in place."

Precision

- *The Man*:
    - "There must be precision in your prayers from this point forward; absolute precision to counter the noise and the violence that will be aimed at the Body. The Church must remember that it is not by might nor by power but by My Spirit that will help you walk straight through the battle. There must be precision and power in your prayers—there *must* be. The war has arrived, and those awake are on the front lines now, and you will never be able to get away from that line. Absolute precision is required in your prayers."
    - "Remember to be precise, as it matters more than ever right now."

"Hail to the Chief"

- *The Man:*
  - "And it all took place in less than 250 years."
  - "Get ready for more than war and speak the truth at risk of the sword."

The Canary in the Coal Mine

- *Jesus*:
  - "Pay attention to details more than you ever have. Go back down with the next crew and be sure to take the canary."
  - "Let the bird out."
- *The Man*:
  - "Somebody has to take the light to the dark places, and there are those who will not like the light that you bring, but they can extinguish the flame that I started in your hearts. Burn brilliantly and with passion; fight the good fight and remain grounded in the Word because the world is about to go dark. And that dark world will need the light you carry to reveal the way to Me."
  - "Go and encourage the crew that is coming down the shaft and tell them I will be working beside them in the dark."

The Headlines, the Sheep, and the Goats

- *The Man:*
  - "Come."
  - "Come."
  - "Get ready to get in line, for I am coming soon. The Spirit and the Bride say 'Come,' and I say 'Soon.'"

Subject Index

Aircraft: 116; 129; 189; 190; 238; 243

Altar: 30; 41; 55; 109

American flag: 87; 92; 104; 205

Biden, Joe: 54; 55; 80; 111; 112; 129; 131; 132

Birds: xiv; xvi; 21; 24; 64; 103; 104; 105; 223; 224; 225; 236; 245

Blood: 4; 31; 54; 71; 91; 98; 104; 112; 115; 116; 132; 135; 136; 140; 146; 153; 172; 173; 202; 210; 238; 241; 244

"Brace" & "Brace Yourself": 21; 24; 27; 47; 51; 55; 57; 60; 64; 72; 84; 94; 100; 117; 121; 125; 132; 142; 150; 159; 163; 168; 173; 190; 211; 228; 229; 233; 234; 235; 236; 237; 238; 239; 240; 241; 243; 244

Capitol Building: 80; 97; 98; 99; 100; 108; 111; 116; 117; 162

Casket: 80

Chains: 109; 123; 161; 162; 163; 240

China: 140; 163; 181; 182; 183; 205; 240

Christians: 4; 14; 15; 31; 42; 63; 64

Church: xvii; xix; xx; 3; 4; 5; 6; 8; 13; 14; 15; 16; 24; 30; 37; 41; 50; 55; 64; 83; 97; 98; 99; 100; 108; 109; 117; 123; 124; 132; 147; 166; 178; 179; 197; 199; 215; 231; 232; 234; 236; 238; 239; 242; 243; 245

Clinton, Hillary: 54; 55

Clouds: 41; 60; 97; 107; 158; 166; 167; 205; 206; 207

Clowns: 51

Congressmen: 116

Dark figure: 37; 38

Dragon: 163; 181; 182; 183; 240; 242

Elected figures: 46; 49; 92; 193; 116; 221

Finger: xiv; xv; 21; 23; 49; 53; 54; 57; 63

Fire: xiii; 4; 10; 13; 14; 15; 21; 24; 42; 49; 53; 55; 64; 71; 80; 94; 116; 125; 136; 137; 140; 141; 142; 146; 147; 149; 150; 166; 167; 174; 178; 179; 181; 184; 198; 202; 215; 220; 236; 238; 239; 241; 242

Firecrackers: 49

Fist: 23; 99

Goats: 227; 228; 246

God: xiii; xiv; xv; xvi; xviii; xix; xx; 3; 4; 5; 6; 7; 8; 9; 10; 11; 12; 13; 14; 15; 16; 23; 30; 31; 33; 38; 77; 84; 87; 88; 91; 93; 123; 124; 125; 146; 147; 149; 154; 229; 230; 231; 232; 233; 236; 238

Hand: 21; 23; 41; 42; 87; 99; 153

Harris, Kamala: 54; 55; 131

Headlines: 21; 45; 46; 53; 54; 59; 63; 64; 206; 214; 227; 228; 229; 246

Israel: xv; xvi; 140; 141

Jesus: xx; 6; 8; 10; 11; 12; 13; 14; 15; 41; 42; 63; 64; 77; 109; 146; 150; 223; 224; 245

Lincoln, Abraham: 91; 92; 93; 94; 236

The Man: xv; xvi; xviii; 6; 72; 81; 84; 94; 99; 100; 104; 105; 107; 108; 109; 115; 117; 120; 125; 126; 132; 137; 141; 142; 145; 146; 147; 149; 150; 158; 163; 166; 168; 173; 174; 178; 179; 183; 190; 199; 202; 203; 207; 210; 211; 215; 221; 224; 225; 228; 233; 235; 236; 237; 238; 239; 240; 241; 242; 243; 244; 245; 246

Masks: 21; 83; 104; 125

Subject Index

Midwest: 202; 210

Military: 7; 24; 119; 120; 140; 183; 205; 206; 213; 220; 221

Money: 24; 27; 50; 99; 116; 137

Oval Office: 119; 120; 132; 135

Rats: 135; 136; 238

Red: 29; 30; 75; 80; 97; 99; 104; 119; 125; 132; 163; 178; 181; 182; 183; 189; 205; 213; 240

Pastors/Preachers: 5; 29; 31; 50; 97; 109; 149; 150

Prayer: xiv; xv; xvi; xviii; 5; 7; 34; 41; 42; 50; 107; 109; 124; 153; 203; 215; 231; 244; 245

Russia: 24; 140; 141; 193; 206

Secret Service: 55; 132; 219; 220

Senators: 80; 97; 116; 161

Sheep: 227; 228; 229; 246

Ships: 33; 34; 63; 137; 205; 206; 213; 239

Soldiers: xvii; 24; 76; 77; 105; 120; 177; 178; 193; 214; 220

Trees: xvii; 53; 71; 124

Trump, Donald: 24; 53; 54; 55; 116

Ukraine: 193; 206

Uncle Sam: 91; 92; 93; 94; 236

Washington, D.C.: 24; 46; 54; 80; 115; 117; 119; 162; 228

White Figure: 21; 23; 24; 46; 51; 57; 60; 64; 72; 233; 234; 235

White House: 80; 81; 119; 120; 136; 162; 229

Winter: 31; 59; 63; 64; 71; 116; 123; 178; 181; 182; 193; 194; 235; 243

Wolves: 29; 30; 31; 124; 125; 149; 177; 179

Simply Dreaming

Calendar Months Of:

January 2020: 21; 71
February 2020: 21
March 2020: xiv; xvii; 21
April 2020: 21
May 2020: 21
June 2020: xiv; xvi; xvii, 21; 23; 27; 29; 33; 37
July 2020: xix; 23; 37; 41; 45
August 2020: 23; 45; 49; 53; 57; 59; 63
September 2020: xiv; 23; 41; 42; 63; 67; 71; 75
October 2020: 23; 49; 79; 83; 236
November 2020: 23; 53; 59; 87; 91; 235
December 2020: 45; 63; 80
January 2021: 103; 107; 111; 115
May 2021: 21; 104; 145
June 2021: 140; 149; 153; 157; 158
July 2021: 140; 161
August 2021: 140; 165
September 2021: 140; 171
January 2022: 189; 193
February 2022: 189; 197
March 2022: 189; 201
April 2022: 189; 205
May 2022: 189; 209
June 2022: 189; 213
July 2022: 189; 213
August 2022: 189; 219
September 2022: 189

www.ingramcontent.com/pod-product-compliance
Lightning Source LLC
Chambersburg PA
CBHW071336080526
44587CB00017B/2859